ONE BALL KNITS

Accessories

ONE BALL KNITS

Accessories

20 Stylish Designs Made with a Single Ball,
Skein, Hank, or Spool

Fatema, Khadija, and Hajera Habibur-Rahman

WATSON-GUPTILL PUBLICATIONS

NEW YORK

Executive Editor: Joy Aquilino
Editor: Martha Moran
Copy Editor: Daryl Brower
Technical Editor: Laura Polley
Designer: Interior design by 3+Co. (www.threeandco.com)
Production Director: Alyn Evans
Photography: Matthew Sandager, Bill Milne
Illustrations: Carmen Galiano

First published in 2008 by Watson-Guptill Publications
an imprint of the Crown Publishing Groups
a division of Random House, Inc., New York
www.crownpublishing.com
www.watsonguptill.com

ISBN-13: 978-0-8230-3322-5
ISBN-10: 0-8230-3322-8

Library of Congress Control Number: 2007937858

Printed in China

First printing, 2007
2 3 4 5 6 7 8 9 / 15 14 13 12 11 10 09

Special dedication and love to our mother and father, who have gently guided us throughout our lives. We are eternally grateful to be blessed with our wonderful parents.

To our beloved brother Mustofa for his words of encouragement and advice. Your firm belief in our potential has greatly inspired us.

To Mohammed Alam, for his constant care and support.

To our sweet Abdulah and lovely Aasiya, whose endearing dimpled smiles and toothy grins always keep us in high spirits.

To all our family and friends for their sound advice and willingness to encourage us in our endeavors.

And last but not least, to all knitters whose stash of yarn is endless.

ACKNOWLEDGMENTS

We are very grateful to everyone at Watson-Guptill Publications who helped us make this book.

First, we would like to thank our publisher, Amy Rhodes. Special thanks to our editor, Joy Aquilino—we so appreciate all your time and effort in guiding us throughout the process of creating this book. Your advice and encouragement helped bring our vision into reality. Many thanks to our project editor, Martha Moran, for your helpful tips, notes, and advice when editing our manuscript, and to our copy editor, Daryl Brower, for making sure we were clear and precise in our writing.

We cannot thank you enough, Gabriele Wilson and Timothy Hsu, for all your consideration and creativity in designing our book. Under your direction, our words and patterns have truly turned into a work of "art." Many thanks to the designers at 3+Co. for the beautiful interior design. We truly appreciate your work. Additionally, we would like to thank Mathew Sandager for your elegant photography and eagerness to provide us with pictures that would please us. Thanks also to Bill Milne for your detailed photos. To our illustrator, Carmen Galiano, thank you for the clear and accurate illustrations that complement our work, making our words come "alive" to our readers. We would also like to thank our technical editor, Laura Polley, for ensuring our patterns are accurate.

Special thanks to the many companies who contributed the supplies we needed to create the designs in this book. Their generous support is greatly valued and deeply appreciated.

Jennifer Orr from Alpaca With A Twist; Carol Mucha at Artistic Wire; Tom Ware and Wendy Lacy from BagWorks; Margery Winter and Deana Gavioli from Berroco; Judy Wilson and Kim Schlager from Brown Sheep Co.; Kathleen Sams and Terri Geck from Coats & Clark; Claudia Langmaid and Kristina Good from Unique Kolours; Ursula Maletz at Joseph Galler Yarns; Irina Germash from Lion Brand Yarns; Ketsia Poteau from M&J Trimming; Dave, Marlene Peden, and Melissa Americano from Pure Allure; Cheryl Schaefer and Laura Nelkin from the Schaefer Yarn Company; Josie Dolan from S.R. Kertzer; Nancy Thomas and Nicole Maiorino from Tahki•Stacy Charles, Inc.; Dana Jones from Tandy Leather Company; Jessica Valentine from Westminster Fibers; and Terri Seiden and Tiffany Guidice from Westrim Crafts.

Without our family and friends, it would have been very hard to reach this far.

Our heartfelt thanks also goes out to Maulana Mehtar and Aunty for their guidance and direction whenever needed. Dearest Faatimah and Maseeha, we are grateful for your kind words and input.

CONTENTS

INTRODUCTION

How many creative possibilities are contained in just one ball of yarn? More than you might think. With this book we set out to explore just what could be done with a single skein, stretching our creativity and experimenting with design, technique, embellishment, and stitch pattern. The result was a collection of twenty attractive, elegant accessories—ponchos, socks, hats, handbags, and more—all crafted from just one ball of yarn and as much fun to make as they are to wear. Most were designed with the advanced beginner in mind, but we've also included a few more challenging designs for those who want to expand their knitting skills. You can use the yarns we suggest or draw a beautiful ball from your own stash (refer to the section on substituting yarns on page 13, first).

For us, designing with just one ball of yarn was both enjoyable and a bit challenging. As sisters, we have many things in common, especially our passion for knitting. But we each have our own approach to the craft—and our own unique style. Each project required a compromise in taste and opinions to create one perfect design. Most of the time we managed to find common ground; when we couldn't, we turned (as always) to our mom for her sound opinions and advice. Drawing on our Eastern heritage, we incorporated traditional stitches, such as those in the classic Turkish Wrap on page 102, and ethnic designs, such as the Panja on page 42. We have included many traditional American styles as well, such as the Western Belt on page 48 and the Cropped Vest on page 92. The inspiration for each project differed, but we had one goal in mind for all of them—to give you a variety of looks and styles that will complement any wardrobe. We enjoyed designing these accessories and we hope you find equal enjoyment in knitting and wearing them as well. Wishing you all a happy knitting experience.

Fatema, Khadija, and Hajera

ONE BALL BASICS

YARN

Yarn is the essential element of any knitting project and there are ever-increasing varieties available today. To help you figure out which one is right for your project, you'll need a basic understanding of the different types. Yarns are classified into three fiber categories: animal, plant, and synthetic. Animal fibers are derived from various animal coats, including sheep (wool), goats (mohair and cashmere), alpacas, rabbits, and even buffalo. Fibers in the plant category include cotton, linen, bamboo, soy, and cellulose-derived fibers such as viscose and rayon. Synthetic fibers are created from manmade materials and include acrylic, nylon, and polyester.

The majority of yarns you'll encounter are sold as hanks, balls, skeins. Balls and skeins are ready to use as is, but hanks must be wound into balls before you knit. You can do this by hand or use a ball winder or swift. Cones and spools are large windings of yarn on cardboard or plastic tubes and are usually used on knitting machines.

Hang on to the label (also called the ball band) wrapped around the yarn. This lists the yarn's fiber content, the dye lot number, the length of the yarn in yards or meters, care and washing instructions, and any special processing done to the yarn. Most labels also provide the recommended knitting gauge (see page 17) for the yarn and the needle size needed to achieve it.

YARN WEIGHTS

In knitting terms, weight refers to the thickness of the yarn, rather than how it tips the scale. Yarn weight falls into seven categories: Lace (33–40 stitches over 4 inches), Superfine (27–32 stitches over 4 inches), Fine (23–26 stitches), Light (21–24 stitches), Medium (16–20 stitches), Bulky (12–15 stitches), and Super Bulky (6–11 stitches). The thicker the

Ball

Skein

Hank

Photographs by Bill Milne

yarn strand, the fewer stitches you'll knit to the inch; the thinner the yarn strand, the more stitches in an inch.

YARN WEIGHT CATEGORIES

Types of yarn in category Knit gauge range (St st to 4 inches) Recommended needle sizes

Fingering, 10-count crochet thread • 33–40 sts • #000–1/1.5–2.5mm

Sock, fingering, baby • 27–32 sts • #1-3/2.25-3.25mm

Sport, baby • 23–26 sts • #3-5/3.25-3.75mm

DK, light worsted • 21–24 sts • #5-7/3.75-4.5mm

Worsted, afghan, aran • 16–20 sts • #7-9/4.5-5.5mm

Chunky, craft, rug • 12–15 sts • #9-11/5.5-8mm

Bulky, roving • 6–11 sts • #11 and larger/8mm and larger

DYE LOTS

Yarns are dyed in batches, called dye lots. Colors may vary slightly from dye lot to dye lot, so to keep the shades in your garment or accessory consistent, you'll want to make certain that all the skeins you purchase for your project have the same dye lot number (you'll find this information on the yarn's ball band or label).

PLY

Yarn is made by spinning fibers into single strands. These strands are then twisted together to create a plied yarn. The ply number on the label refers to the number of yarn strands that were twisted together in that particular ball or skein. Two-ply yarns are made by twisting two strands together, three-ply yarns by twisting three strands together, and so on.

STORAGE

Store your yarn as carefully as you would your clothing. Keep any unused balls, hanks, or skeins in a clean, dust-free area away from direct sunlight, which can cause colors to fade and fibers to break down. Plastic bins with lids, lidded baskets, or zippered canvas sweater bags are all good storage options. You can add cedar blocks or sachets filled with lavender or rosemary to keep moths away.

YARN SUBSTITUTIONS

In each of the instructions for our designs list the specific yarn used in the project. This is the yarn we recommend you use. If you want to use a different yarn, you can do so, but you must first check that the substitute yarn will actually match the gauge of the recommended yarn by knitting a gauge test swatch. You must knit a test swatch even if the substitute yarn is the same weight as the recommended yarn. For more information on gauge and how to knit a test swatch, see page 16.

GAUGE

The gauge measurements in our instructions refer to the number of rows and the number of stitches over 4 inches/10 centimeters of knitting. For detailed information about gauge, see page 16.

TOOLS

There are many knitting tools out there that are either essential to successful knitting or will help make knitting easier and a more rewarding experience. As you develop your skills, you will find more and more ways to take advantage of the wide array of knitting supplies and accessories available. Here are the tools that you will need for the projects in this book.

KNITTING NEEDLES

The knitting needle is your most essential tool. They come in a vast array of sizes and lengths, and can be made from aluminum, wood, bamboo, and plastic, among other materials. For those who knit at night, there are needles with illuminated tips. If speed is your goal, nickel-plated needles may be the choice for you. Other knitters prefer the warm feel of wood and bamboo. It is important to pick the right type of needle for your project and one that suits your personal knitting style. Your needles should help, not hinder, your knitting efforts, so try various styles until you find the one that works best for you. Comfort and ease are essential when knitting.

KNITTING NEEDLE SIZE CHART

Metric Sizes	U.S. Sizes
2 mm	0
2.25 mm	1
2.75 mm	2
3.25 mm	3
3.5 mm	4
3.75 mm	5
4 mm	6
4.5 mm	7
5 mm	8
5.5 mm	9
6 mm	10
6.5 mm	10.5
8 mm	11
9 mm	13
10 mm	15
12.75 mm	17
15 mm	19
19 mm	35
25 mm	50

Circular, Double-Pointed (DPN), and Single-Pointed Needles

There are many varieties of needles to choose from, each with it's own specific use. Straight needles are the most familiar type; they are essentially long sticks with a point on one end and a knob at the other that keeps the stitches from sliding off the needle. They are sold in pairs in a variety of lengths, the most popular being 10 and 14 inches. Circular needles are two straight needles connected by a wire or tube. They also come in varying lengths. They are most often used for knitting hats, socks, and other items in the round, but many knitters also use them to knit flat pieces. Double-pointed needles are short needles with points on both ends. Sold in sets of four or five, they're most often used for small circular projects, turning sock heels, and making I-cord.

Cable Needles and Stitch Holders

Cable needles are short needles with points at both ends that are shaped either like a fishhook or the letter U to prevent stitches from slipping off the needle as you work a cable. When instructed, you will slip stitches onto the cable needle and hold them to the front or the back of the work as you knit the remaining stitches of the cable.

Stitch holders, which resemble long safety pins, are used to hold open neckline or other stitches that will be bound off or worked into the project at a later point. They are available in a variety of sizes, but smaller ones are used most often.

STITCH MARKERS

Stitch markers are small plastic or rubber rings used to remind the knitter when to begin a new round when knitting circularly or to indicate where to increase, decrease, or change stitch patterns. When the instructions indicate the use of a stitch marker, slip the marker onto your right-hand needle and continue knitting as indicated in the pattern. Yarn shops carry a wide variety of stitch markers, but you can easily create your own by tying a contrasting piece of yarn around your needle at the same place you would position the stitch marker.

ROW COUNTERS

Row counters are handy little gadgets that help keep track how many rows of knitting have been completed. Some slip onto knitting needles, while others are handheld. Turn the knob (or click a button) to advance to the next highest number every time you complete a row.

POINT PROTECTORS

This little rubber or plastic cap slips over the points of your needles, protecting the tips and keeping stitches from sliding off. They also prevent the needle points from poking through the lining of your knitting bag.

TAPESTRY NEEDLES

These large-eyed needles with a blunt or rounded tip are used for seaming, weaving, in ends, and embroidering.

TAPE MEASURE

An accurate tape measure is essential for both construction and blocking. Choose a flexible plastic or fiberglass tape marked in both centimeters and inches to accurately measure stitch and gauge and the finished size of your garment pieces.

CROCHET HOOK

A crochet hook is perfect for picking up dropped stitches or attaching fringe. Smaller crochet hooks work best.

PINS

Pins are used to hold and shape the knitted fabric pieces during blocking or to pin together pieces for seaming. Any pin will do, but specially designed blocking pins with a long shank and flat head are more durable and easier to use.

BLOCKING BOARD

For blocking (see page 38), you'll need a flat, padded, and pinnable surface large enough to accommodate a fully flat and smoothed knitted piece. You can purchase a blocking board or simply use a folded towel.

SPRAY BOTTLE

If you use the wet blocking method (see page 38), you will need a spray bottle filled with water.

STEAM IRON OR STEAMER

Steam is required during the steam blocking process (see page 38) and either an iron or a steamer will serve the purpose.

UNDERSTANDING KNITTING INSTRUCTIONS

Knitting instructions have their own vocabulary and terms that are important to understand before you start a project. Here are the knitting terms we use in our instructions.

SKILL LEVEL

We have divided our projects into four different skill levels: Beginner (first-time projects, simple stitches, and minimal shaping), Easy (simple stitches combined with easy stitch changes, color changes, and minimal shaping), Intermediate (a greater variety of stitches, including more complicated lace and cables, double-pointed knitting, color changes, and shaping), and Experienced (advanced knitting techniques, intricate cable and lace stitches, Fair Isle patterns, and shaping). Most of our projects fall under the Beginner and Easy skill levels, but if you feel as a beginner that you can complete an Intermediate project, go for it.

SIZE

Most of our projects are designed for one size. A few are sized Small, Medium, and Large. In these cases measurements are given for each size. (All sample designs were knitted in size Medium.)

FINISHED MEASUREMENTS

This refers to the finished dimensions of the knitted piece, after blocking and assembling.

YARN

This specifies the type of yarn used for the project and the approximate yardage included in the ball or skein

MATERIALS

This list includes all the tools and supplies required to knit the project, including the materials we used to knit our samples.

GAUGE

Gauge refers to the number of stitches and rows per inch of knitting, based on the size of a knitting stitch. The size of the stitch is determined by the yarn and needle size used, and how a particular knitter holds the yarn. In our knitting instructions, gauge is measured over 4 inches/10 centimeters. If your gauge does not precisely match the gauge given in the instructions, you will change the size of your finished piece. It is therefore essential that you check your gauge by knitting a test swatch before starting each project.

Here's an example of how gauge will be stated in our instructions: 16 stitches = 4"/10cm over St st (knit one row, purl next row).

The Gauge Test Swatch

Even if you are using the exact yarn and needles recommended in the instructions, you will need to knit a test swatch to check the gauge. This is because not every knitter controls the yarn in exactly the same way, and you may get a different number of stitches per 4 inches than another knitter, even if you are both using the exact same yarn and needles. Using a yarn other than the one specified in the pattern will also affect gauge and will need to be tested, too.

To make the test swatch, use the same needles and yarn you plan to use for the project, cast on the number of stitches required to get at least 4 inches of knitting (usually 20 or more stitches) and knit several rows until you end up with a swatch that measures at least 4 inches/10 centimeters (4"/10 cm) square. Flatten the swatch, straighten the rows and stitches, and then lay the tape measure on top of the swatch and count the number of stitches and rows as follows:

1. Count the number of stitches across 2"/5cm; multiply results by 2 to get the number of stitches per 4"/10cm.

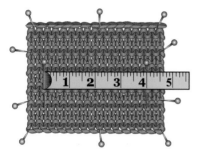

2. Count the number of rows along 2"/5cm, multiply results by 2 to get the number of rows per 4"/10cm.

   If you find that your gauge does not match the gauge given in the instructions, try changing your needles. Larger needles will decrease the number of stitches per inch; smaller needles will increase the number of stitches per inch.

PATTERN NOTES

This section will explain any important information concerning the project, clarifications in the instructions, or variations you might try.

SPECIAL ABBREVIATIONS

Abbreviations are used in written knitting instructions, and we provide a list of any special abbreviations used in each project's instructions, along with their meanings. Below is a list of some of the most commonly used abbreviations.

BO	bind off
CO	cast on
cont	continue; continuing
dec	decrease, decreasing
dpn	double-pointed needle
foll	follow, follows, following
inc	increasing
k	knit
K2tog	knit 2 together
LH	left-hand
p	purl
P2tog	purl 2 together
patt/patts	pattern/patterns
psso	pass slip stitch over
rep	repeat

RH	right-hand
Rnd	round
RS	right side
SKP	slip one, knit one, pass slip stitch over
Ssk	slip, slip, knit
st	stitch
yo	yarn over

STITCH PATTERN(S)

In most cases, stitch pattern(s) used in the project will be presented in both written instruction and in chart form. You will refer to the written instructions and chart(s) when the project instructions call for that specific stitch pattern.

KNITTING INSTRUCTIONS

This is where the knitting instructions for each project begins. We tell you how many stitches to cast on, which stitch pattern to use, and how much to knit or bind off.

CHARTS

In most cases, the written instructions for each stitch pattern are accompanied by charts. These charts are visual representations of the stitch patterns and can sometimes be easier to follow than the line-by-line written instructions.

How to Read Charts

Each chart is accompanied by a legend that explains the meaning of each symbol in the blocks of the chart (i.e., the type of stitch represented in each block). You'll notice that there are numbers running along both the right- and left-hand sides of the chart. These refer to row numbers, for example, the number "1" refers to Row 1. If the numbering begins on the right-hand side of chart, you will start knitting on the right side (RS) of the work. When the numbering begins on left-hand side of chart, you will begin knitting on the wrong side (WS).

In Figure 1 we have a chart that begins with a right-side row. You will notice that the numbering of rows starts on the right. This indicates that you will begin knitting Row 1 from the right, moving to the left. Row 2 instructs you to begin knitting from left to right. In this case you will read all odd-numbered rows from right to left and all even-numbered rows from left to right.

Figure 2 shows a chart that begins on a wrong-side row. Begin following the chart from left to right. On Row 2, you will follow the chart from right to left. In this case you will read all odd-numbered rows from left to right and all even numbered rows from right to left.

Figure 3 shows a chart as it appears in the instructions, complete with stitch symbols. Each chart is accompanied by a legend for the symbols used in the chart, which corresponds to the written instructions.

Row 1 (RS): Skp *yo, k1, yo, k3tog, yo, k1; rep from * to last two sts,
yo, k2tog.

Row 2: Purl
Row 3: *K4, yo, skp; rep from * , to last three sts, k3.
Row 4: Knit

SCHEMATICS AND TEMPLATES

Schematics are line illustrations that show the design, or design piece, laid flat. Schematics are labeled with the name of the piece and the exact measurements that each piece should be when completed.

Templates are flat pattern pieces for cutting shapes out of knit fabric. Our templates appear in the book at their actual size.

Figure 1

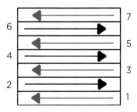

Figure 2

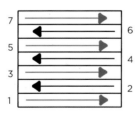

Figure 3

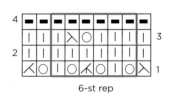

6-st rep

Legend for Figure 3

	Knit on RS, Purl on WS
	Purl on RS, Knit on WS
O	Yarn over
	Skp
	K2tog
	K3tog

KNITTING TECHNIQUES
MAKING A SLIP KNOT

1. Pull out a length of yarn from the ball and form it into a pretzel as shown.

2. Insert the needle under the bar and pull a loop.

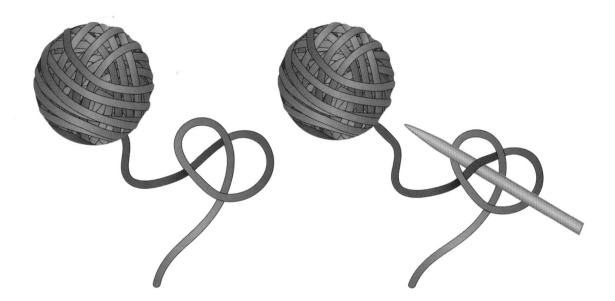

3. Tighten the loop with your thumb and index finger.

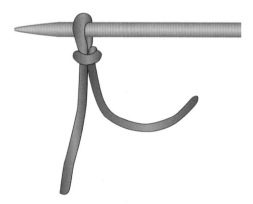

CONTINENTAL LONG TAIL CAST-ON

1. With the slip knot on the needle, wrap the short end of the yarn around your thumb. Wrap the yarn from the ball around your index finger. Hold both ends of the yarn taut in the palm of your hand.

2. Insert the needle into the loop near the thumb and lift it.

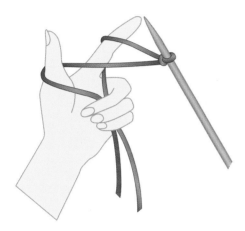

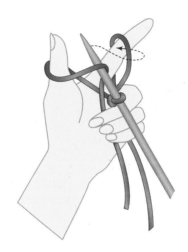

3. Keeping the thumb loop on the needle; slip the needle into the loop from the index finger.

   Pull a new loop through the thumb loop. One stitch is made.

BACKWARD LOOP CAST-ON

1. With the slip knot on the needle, wrap the yarn tail around your thumb, holding the end in the your palm.

2. Insert the needle through the loop from front to back.

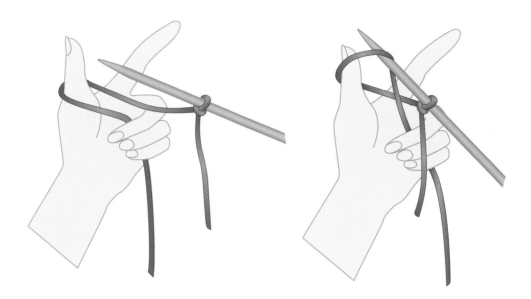

3. Tighten.

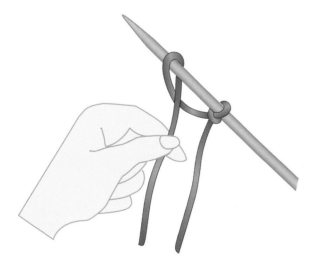

CABLE CAST-ON

1. With the slip knot on the needle, insert the right-hand needle from the front to the back of the stitch. Wrap the yarn from back to front around the needle.

2. Pull the wrapped yarn through the stitch, being sure not to drop the worked stitch off the left-hand needle.

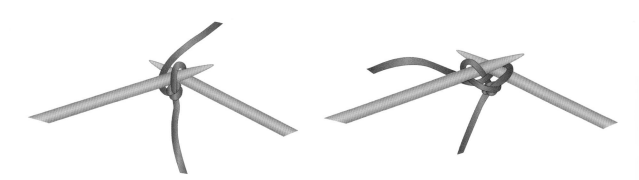

3. Slip the stitch from the right-hand needle to left-hand needle. Two stitches are on the left-hand needle.

KNIT STITCH

1. Keeping the yarn in back, insert the right-hand needle from the front into the back of the first stitch.

2. Wrap the yarn around the needle from back to front once.

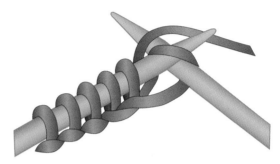

3. Pull the wrapped yarn through the first stitch.

4. Keep the new stitch on the right-hand needle; drop the first stitch from the left-hand needle.

PURL STITCH

1. Keeping the yarn in front between the two needles, insert the right-hand needle from the back to the front of the first stitch on the left-hand needle. Wrap the yarn around the stitch on the right-hand needle from back to front once.

2. Pull the wrapped yarn through the back.

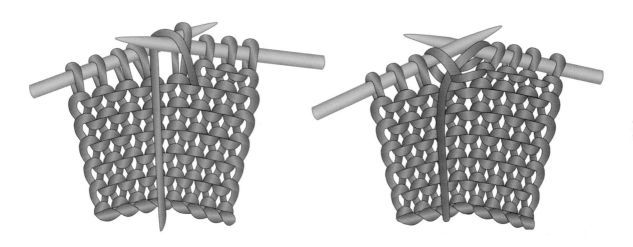

3. Keep the new stitch on the right-hand needle; drop the first stitch from the left-hand needle.

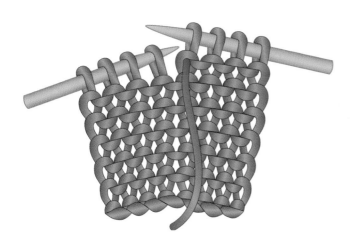

SLIP STITCH KNITWISE

Insert the right-hand needle through the stitch
as if to knit. Slide the stitch off the left needle
and onto the right needle without working
the stitch.

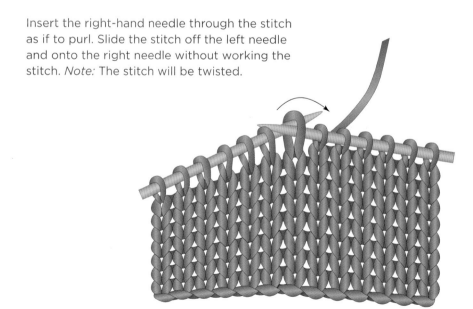

SLIP STITCH PURLWISE

Insert the right-hand needle through the stitch
as if to purl. Slide the stitch off the left needle
and onto the right needle without working the
stitch. *Note:* The stitch will be twisted.

YARN OVER BETWEEN KNIT STITCHES

1. Bring the yarn forward between the two needles and lift it over the right-hand needle.

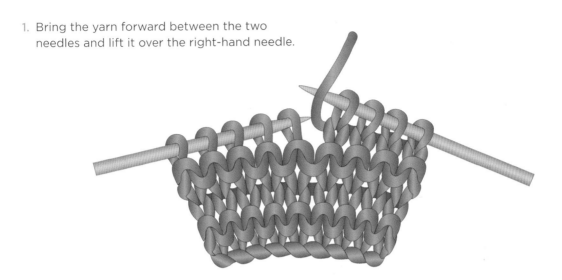

2. Knit the next stitch, bringing the yarn to the back over the right needle and producing a loop before the knitted stitch.

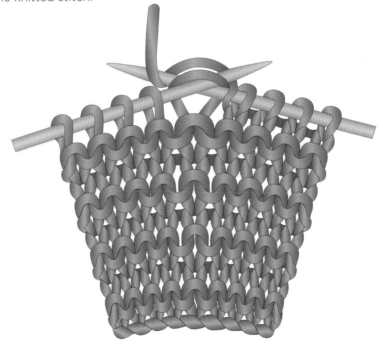

YARN OVER BETWEEN PURL STITCHES

Leave the yarn in the front of the work and wrap it around the right-hand needle once. Purl the next stitch. (See the Purl Stitch instructions on page 25.)

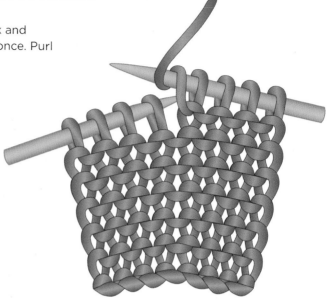

INCREASE (KNITTING INTO THE FRONT AND BACK LOOP)

1. Knit into the front loop of the stitch without dropping the worked stitch from the left-hand needle.

2. Knit into the back loop of the same stitch. Drop the worked stitch from the left-hand needle. Two stitches are on the right-hand needle.

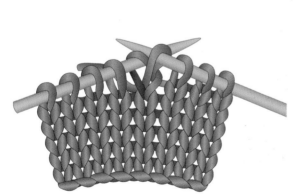

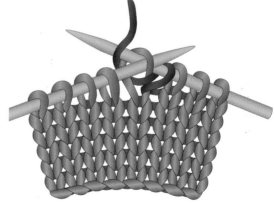

DECREASE (SLIP1, K1, PSSO, OR SKPO)

1. Insert the right-hand needle into the first stitch as if to knit, and slip it onto the needle.

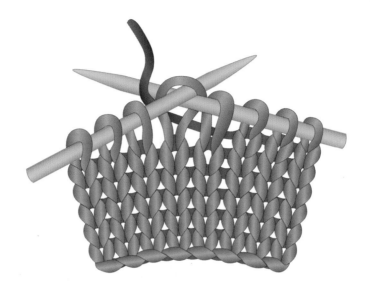

2. Knit the next stitch. Pass the slip stitch over the knit stitch.

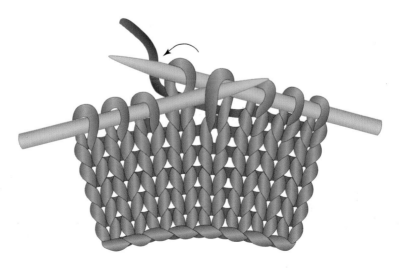

KNITTING CABLES

1. Slip three stitches purlwise onto the cable needle. Hold the cable needle in front of the work.

2. Knit the next three stitches on the left-hand needle, continuing to hold the cable needle in front of the work.

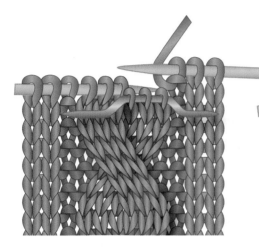

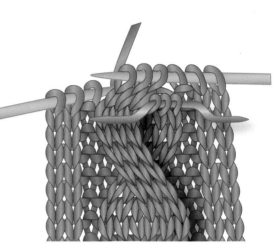

3. Knit the three stitches directly from the cable needle. If it's easier for you, you can return the stitches to the left-hand needle and then knit them. The cable has now been made.

Note: These illustrations show how to make a front, or left, cable. To make a back, or right, cable you follow the same three steps, but you'll hold the cable needle in back of the work, instead of in front of it.

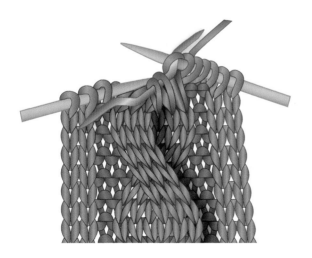

PICKING UP STITCHES

1. Working along the bound-off edge, insert the needle through the center of the first stitch. Wrap the yarn around the needle as if to knit.

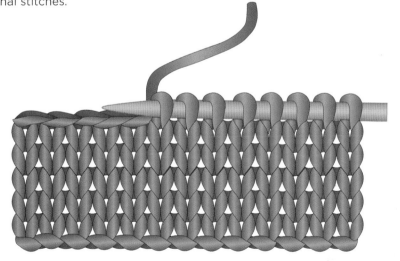

2. To "pick up" a stitch, pull the yarn through the stitch. Repeat to pick up additional stitches.

KNITTING I-CORD

Cast on the number of stitches directed in the instructions. * Knit across the cast-on stitches. Without turning the work, slip the stitches back onto the left-hand needle; repeat from * until you have reached the desired length.

BINDING OFF

Knit 2 stitches. *Insert the left-hand needle into the first knit stitch on the right-hand needle. Lift this stitch over the second stitch and off the needle; repeat from * to the end.

PICKING UP DROPPED STITCHES

Work to the drop stitch. Using a small crochet hook, insert it into the dropped loop hooking to the bar above it. Pull the bar through dropped the stitch. Continue to ladder upwards by pulling the bar through the stitch below.

STRINGING BEADS

Cut a small length of thread. Thread a sewing needle then knot the ends of thread. Slip the end of the yarn through the loop of thread. Slip beads from the needle through the strand of thread and onto the yarn strand.

WHIPSTITCH

Thread a tapestry needle with yarn. With either the right or the wrong side of the fabric facing you, insert the tapestry needle through both fabrics toward you.

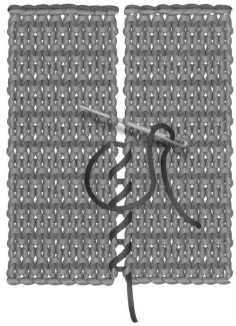

CIRCULAR KNITTING (KNITTING IN THE ROUND)

Cast on a number of stitches. Begin knitting in the round until you reach the first cast-on stitch. With the cast-on edges facing inward, place the marker and knit the first cast-on stitch. Tighten the stitch and proceed knitting the next round.

KNITTING WITH DOUBLE-POINTED NEEDLES

1. Cast on a number of stitches on a single-pointed needle. Slip the cast on stitches evenly on three or four double-pointed needles.

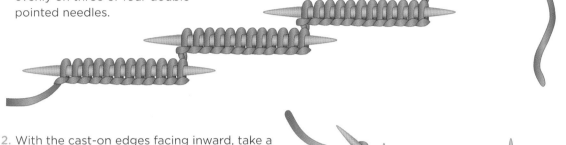

2. With the cast-on edges facing inward, take a free needle and knit the first cast-on stitch. Tighten the stitch and proceed to knit.

MATTRESS STITCH

Knit side (shown): Place the garment pieces you will be joining side by side on a flat surface with the knit side facing up. Insert the needle behind the horizontal bar of the knit stitch on the right-side edge of one garment piece. Repeat the same for the left-side edge of the other garment piece. Continue joining the pieces, stitching left and right edges together. Purl side: Place the garment pieces to be joined side by side on a flat surface with the purl side facing up. Insert the needle under one horizontal bar of the purl stitch on the right-side edge of one garment piece, then repeat the same for the left-side edge on the other garment piece.

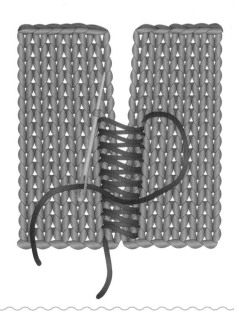

INVISIBLE HORIZONTAL SEAM

With the right sides of the fabric aligned together, insert the needle behind 1 stitch on one
side of the fabric and then behind 1 stitch on
the other fabric piece. Continue in this pattern.

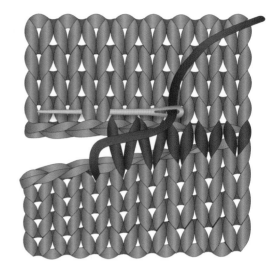

KITCHENER STITCH

Keep the stitches on the needles and the front
needle parallel to the back needle. Insert the
tapestry needle through the first stitch on
the front needle as you would to knit. Slip the
stitch off the needle. Insert the needle through
the next stitch on the front needle as you
would to purl. Leave the stitch on the needle.
Insert the needle through the first stitch on
the back needle as if to purl. Slip the stitch
off the needle. Insert the needle through the
next stitch on the back needle as if to knit.
Leave the stitch on the needle. Repeat steps
1 through 4 until one stitch remains. Pull the
thread through loop.

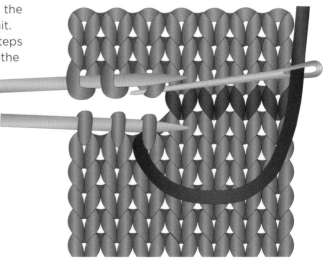

BUTTONHOLE STITCH

Keep the yarn over the edge of the fabric; the beginning of the yarn loop is made. Insert a tapestry needle (1/2"/1.25 cm or desired length) above the fabric edge. Pull the needle behind the fabric and above the beginning yarn loop. Keep the yarn loop below the needle and pull the needle taut. Repeat this procedure all along the edge of the fabric, keeping the yarn loop below the needle throughout.

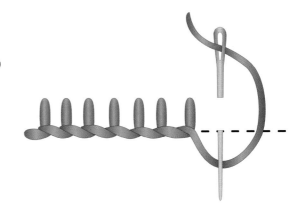

ADDING FRINGE

We have an easy way to prepare fringe so that the fringe is always a consistent length.

1. Cut out a piece of cardboard, making the width of the cardboard equal to the desired length of the fringe.

2. Wrap the yarn around the cardboard the number of times indicated in the pattern instructions (different patterns will tell you to wrap it a different number of times). Cut through the yarn along the bottom edge of the cardboard.

3. Remove the fringe from the cardboard and fold it in half, keeping the bottom edges even.

4. Insert a crochet hook from the back to the front of the garment, and then hook it onto the center of the folded fringe. Draw the yarn loop through the edge of the garment. Slip the fringe tail through the loop and tug tightly to secure it.

5. Trim the edges of the fringe if necessary.

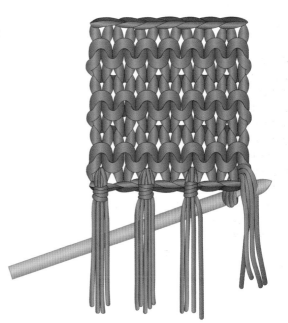

FINISHING

Properly finishing your project is as vital to a successful outcome as the actual knitting. In this section we give you instructions for seaming, blocking, and adding embellishments to your projects.

SEAMING

We seamed most of the garments in the book using the mattress stitch. It provides a clean seamless look to your fabric. Instructions for executing the mattress stitch are on page 35.

BLOCKING

Blocking is an essential step in the construction process. In it the finished knit pieces are steamed or dampened and smoothed into shape, ensuring the exact measurements for the project have been met and that all the rows and stitches are straight and even. There are two methods for achieving this—wet blocking and steam blocking.

In *wet blocking*, the garment is laid flat, smoothed, and straightened and then is pinned down according to the project's finished measurements on a blocking pad or any padded surface. Once you are sure the rows and stitches are flat, even, and straight, and the measurements are exactly correct, fill a spray bottle with water and wet the top side of the piece. Leave the piece pinned in place until it is completely dry. Alternately, you can wet the piece before pinning by holding it under running water or submerging it in a filled sink or basin. Gently squeeze any excess water out of the piece (do not wring), then place it on your blocking pad and pin it to the project measure-

ments. Allow to the piece to air-dry completely before unpinning.

Steam blocking involves the use of an iron. Pin the knit piece(s) on a padded surface according to the finished measurement(s) listed in the instructions, straightening and evening all stitches and rows. Adjust the iron's heat setting according to the fiber content of the yarn used. Place the iron several inches above the knit fabric when steaming. Do not allow the iron to touch the knitted fabric. If you do, you risk scorching the yarn or flattening stitches.

Wet blocking (left) and steam blocking (right)

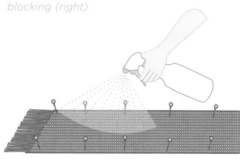
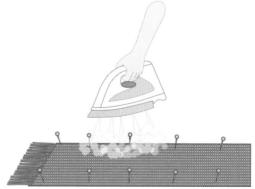

FELTING

Felting is a process that completely changes the texture, size, and feel of knitted wool fabric by altering the fibers so that you can no longer see the individual stitches and rows. (It also shrinks the overall size of the knitted fabric.) *Note:* While felting does shrink the size of the knitted piece, shrinking is not what creates the felted surface. The resulting fabric is thicker, more velvety, and warmer than the original knitted fabric, and it can be cut and sewn in a variety of ways because it won't unravel or lose stitches. Felting works particularly well for appliqués, hats, and bags.

Felting is a lot of fun, and easy to do, particularly when applied to fabrics knit with big needles (i.e., bigger, looser stitches.) Felting projects usually instruct you to use needles two or more sizes larger than the yarn label recommends. Felting is accomplished by subjecting the knitted piece to hot soapy water (which opens up the scales on wool fiber), then agitating the piece to cause the fibers to tangle together. When the piece cools and dries, the scales close up, locking the wool into thick, durable fabric that won't unravel. Felting can be done with a washing machine or by hand. *Note:* Make sure your knitted edges are finished, ends are woven in securely, and that all seams have been stitched before you begin the felting process. Otherwise, you'll create a big mess.

Machine Felting

Felting by washing machine is the easiest and most reliable method. Place the knitted fabric in a washer using a low level of hot water and small amount of laundry detergent (no bleach!). Machine wash the knitted fabric along with a denim garment (one that won't bleed), or inside a zipped pillowcase, for seven to ten minutes. The denim (or pillowcase) creates extra friction in the machine, which speeds up the felting process. Avoid using towels, as they will shed fibers that will be picked up by your felted fabric. Check the fabric periodically, before you reach the "spin" cycle, to see if it has felted. You'll know it's ready when the knitted stitches and rows are no longer visible. Some yarns take longer to felt than others do, so don't worry if your fabric hasn't felted in 10 minutes. Just keep it in the wash cycle and keep checking every few minutes. When the fabric reaches the desired felting, machine rinse it in cool water, and then spin on gentle (never wring the fabric). Remove the fabric from the washing machine (you will notice that it has shrunk significantly from its original size), lay it flat, and gently straighten and shape it, leaving it to air-dry. Remember that if you don't like your finished result, you can always felt it some more. (You can't, however, unfelt that which has already been felted.)

Hand Felting

Soak knitted fabric in a bowl (or sink or tub) filled with hot water for 30 minutes. Add a small amount of laundry detergent to the water and hand wash it, rubbing the fabric together until you reach your desired felting. Rinse the felted fabric under cold water to stop the felting process. Squeeze out the excess water (never wring), and then lay the fabric flat, shape it, and leave it out to air-dry.

CARING FOR YOUR KNITTED ACCESSORIES

Wash the finished design according to the instructions on the yarn label. Knitted garments are usually laid flat and air-dried, unless otherwise indicated on label.

ONE BALL PATTERNS

PANJA (HAND JEWELRY)

Our knit *panja* was inspired by the traditional Indian hand jewelry worn by women from the Indian subcontinent on special occasions such as weddings and religious holidays. Traditionally made from 22k gold, the panja is designed to accent the delicate qualities of the hand. In our interpretation, we used a simple lace stitch and small beads to create the same effect in a modern, feminine, and flattering fashion accessory.

SKILL LEVEL
Easy

SIZE
One size

FINISHED MEASUREMENTS
Base: 6"/15.2cm
including clasps
Height: 5"/12.7cm

YARN
1 ball Twilley Washable Gold-fingering (80% viscose/20% metallized polyester, .875oz/25 g = approx 108 yd/98.8m per ball) in #58 Burgundy OR approx 12 yd/11m viscose/metallized polyester blend, fingering-weight yarn

MATERIALS
- Size 5 U.S. (3.75mm) straight and double-pointed needles or size to obtain gauge
- 1 package Westrim Crafts size 6/o silver-lined gold rochaille beads Style #4997-4 OR 55 size 6/o glass beads in gold
- 1 spool of Artistic Wire #S-30S-03-30YD gold (30 gauge, 30 yd/27.5m) OR 2 yards (5m) of 30 gauge gold jewelry wire, to attach clasp
- 1 package Hirschberg Schutz Better Beads 2-strand Fili-gree Box Clasps in gold OR 1 set 2-strand filigree box clasps, which can be pur-chased at any craft store.

- Size 18-22 chenille sewing needle, for weaving the ends of loose yarn strands and attaching clasps to the band
- Sewing thread in burgundy (Optional: can be used instead of jewelry wire to attach clasp)

GAUGE
28 sts = 4"/10cm over St st
Always take time to check your gauge.

PATTERN NOTES
- Right side of panja will have the stitches slanted right. After the panja is completed, the band will be worked next. Clasps will be attached to both ends of band. Work yo with bead when referred to.
- Both chart and written instructions for Panja Lace Stitch patt are provided. Choose the instruction method you prefer.
- For instructions on working I-cord, see page 32.
- For casting on sts at the beginning of band, see page 21.

SPECIAL ABBREVIATIONS
K2tog: Knit two stitches together.
yo: Yarn over
yob: Yarn over with bead

STITCH PATTERN
Panja Lace Stitch (over 3 sts, increased to 22 sts)
Row 1 (RS): K1, yob, k2tog. (3 sts)
Row 2 and all WS rows: Yo, purl across (one st increased)
Row 3: K1, yob, k2tog, yob, k1. (5 sts)
Row 5: K1, [yob, k2tog] twice, yob, k1. (7 sts)
Row 7: K1, [yob, k2tog] 3 times, yob, k1. (9 sts)
Row 9: K1, [yob, k2tog] 4 times, yob, k1. (11 sts)
Row 11: K1, [yob, k2tog] 5 times, yob, k1. (13 sts)
Row 13: K1, [yob, k2tog] 6 times, yob, k1. (15 sts)
Row 15: K1, [yob, k2tog] 7 times, yob, k1. (17 sts)
Row 17: K1, [yob, k2tog] 8 times, yob, k1. (19 sts)
Row 19: K1, [yob, k2tog] 9 times, yob, k1. (21 sts)
Row 20: Yo, purl across. (22 sts)
Work Rows 1–20 once for Panja Lace Stitch patt.

SEED STITCH
Row 1: Purl the knit sts and knit the purl sts.
Rep Row 1 for Seed St.

PANJA
Make 1.
String 55 beads onto yarn. Cast on 3 stitches. Work in I-cord for 3"/7.6cm. Keep 3 sts on RH needle. Insert RH needle through the cast-on

STITCH CHART
(Panja Lace Stitch) (3 sts, increased to 22 sts)

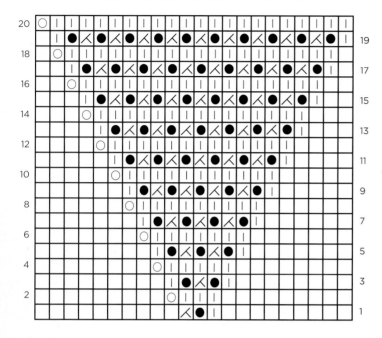

Legend

I	Knit on RS, Purl on WS
●	Yarn over with bead
⋏	K2tog
○	Yarn over

Work Rows 1–20 once

edge of the I-cord, picking up 3 stitches. (6 sts on RH needle)
Next row (WS): (K2tog) across. (3 sts)
Begin Panja Lace patt.

Band
Next Row: Cast on 5 sts at the beginning of row. *K1, p1; rep from * to last st, k1. (27 sts)
Next Row: Cast on 5 sts at the beginning of row. *P1, k1; rep from * across. (32 sts)
Work Seed St for 5 more rows. Bind off all sts.

Attaching Clasp
With thin wire or thread, attach clasps on both ends of the band.

FINISHING
Weave in ends.

DESIGN TIP
Make two, one for each hand. *Note:* You knit the Panja the same way for either hand. No shaping is necessary.

CRYSTAL BEAD NECKLACE AND EARRINGS

This design is our modern interpretation of the traditional Indian jhumka, an earring first created during the royal Mughal Empire. The name refers to the bell or chandelier shape of the earring, which is a traditional style worn at weddings, festivals, and other special occasions on the Indian subcontinent. Our own design was inspired by the feminine elegance and grace of the original, and we carried that inspiration into the necklace design. Though our design is no less elegant than the original, it is very easy to make, requiring only knit and slip stitches.

SKILL LEVEL
Easy

SIZE
One size

FINISHED MEASUREMENTS
Necklace: 12"/30.5cm long for each strand A and B 3"/33cm long for strand C
Earrings: 1¼"/3.1cm (including beaded head) x ¾"/1.9cm

WIRE
1 spool of Artistic Wire (30 gauge/30yds), #S-30S-03-30YD (30 yd/27.5m) in gold OR approx 30 yds, 30 gauge jewelry wire

MATERIALS (FOR ALL PIECES)
• Size 5 U.S. (3.75mm) needles or size to obtain gauge
• 1 package each Pure Allure Crystal Innovations, 4mm Swarovski Crystal Beads (32 pcs) in White Opal and Blue Zircon OR 24 4mm crystal beads in white and 29
• 4mm crystal beads in turquoise blue
• 1 package of Gold Elegance 14k Gold Plate Sm Ball Hooked Wire #29497-27 (8 pcs) OR 2 small hooked earring wires

• 1 package Hirschberg Schutz & Co., Inc. Elite Better Beads, clasp, #BB3678-02 in gold (which can be found in any craft store) OR 1 3-strand tube with lobster clasp

PATTERN NOTES
• The earrings are knitted with the beads. The wire easily snaps off, so take care not to knit tightly.
• To knit with bead, knit the indicated st with the bead pushed forward.
• For instructions on working the Backward Loop Cast-On, see page 22.

NECKLACE
Strand A
Slip 11 beads alternately onto wire beginning with blue until there are 6 blue and 5 white beads.
Cast on 1 stitch.
*[(Knit 1 stitch slightly loose. Turn four times. Knit with bead;] rep from * until all beads are knitted, ending [(Knit 1 stitch slightly loose. Turn) 4 times]. Break wire and pull through loop. Tighten. Set aside.

Strand B
Slip 9 beads alternately onto wire beginning with blue until there are 5 blue and 4 white beads.
Cast on 1 stitch.
*[(Knit 1 stitch slightly loose. Turn) 5 times. Knit with bead;]

rep from * until all beads are knitted, ending [(Knit 1 stitch slightly loose. Turn) 5 times]. Break wire and pull through loop. Tighten. Set aside.

Strand C
Slip 8 beads alternately onto wire beginning with blue until there are 4 blue and 4 white beads.
Cast on 1 stitch.
*[(Knit 1 stitch slightly loose. Turn) 6 times. Knit with bead;] rep from * until all beads are knitted, ending [(Knit 1 stitch slightly loose. Turn) 6 times]. Break wire and pull through loop. Tighten. Set aside.

ATTACHING NECKLACE TO CLASP
Slip wire end from cast on edge of Strand A through first hole of one clasp several times to fasten. Attach opposite end of Strand A to the first hole of second clasp. Attach ends of Strand B to second hole on both clasps in the same manner. Attach ends of Strand C to third hole on both clasps in the same manner.

EARRINGS
Make 2
Break off 2"/5cm of wire, set aside. Cast on 16 stitches using the Backward Loop Cast-On. Knit 3 rows.

Row 4: K1, (k2tog) 7 times, k1. (9 stitches remain)
Row 5: K1, (k2tog) 4 times. (5 stitches remain)
Row 6: K1, (k2tog) twice. (3 stitches remain)
Row 7: Slip 1 stitch, knit 1 stitch, pass slipped stitch over the knit stitch and off the needle. (1 stitch remains).

Seaming Sides

Keep st on needle, without breaking wire. With the 2"/5cm of wire you set aside earlier, sew slanted sides of earring together. Shape earring with your little finger, forming a small chandelier. Repeat for other earring.

Beaded Head and Edging

Keeping loop on needle, pull out more wire until the loop is 1/2"/1.27 cm longer. Remove loop from needle and flatten the loop carefully, pinching the sides of the loop together to narrow the opening. Slip 1 blue, 1 white, and 1 blue bead onto the flattened loop. Cut attached wire, leaving a 2"/5cm tail. Slip 1 blue, 1 white, and 1 blue bead onto the snapped tail. Slip tail through the opening of the flattened loop above the beads. Slip 1 blue, 1 white, and 1 blue bead onto the same wire and twist wire end around the top of chandelier (below beaded head) to fasten. Slightly unflatten loop and place earring hook through the loop. Break off 1/2"/1.27 cm wire and fasten to earring hook and twist above beaded head of chandelier. With knitting needle, poke through the knitted holes on the earrings, making them uniform.

Beaded Edge on Earring

Break off 3"/7.6cm of wire. *Slip wire from WS to RS through front loop of 1 st of cast-on edge of earring. Place 1 blue bead onto wire, slip wire through the back loop of same st (1 beaded loop); repeat from * into each st around cast-on edge, alternating white and blue beads until each st is beaded and there are 8 blue and 8 white beads around edge. Break off extra wire and fasten through edge of earring. Repeat for other earring.

FINISHING
Weave in ends.

DESIGN TIP
Pick your favorite colored beads to match your wardrobe.

WESTERN BELT

Our interpretation of the classic western belt will enhance many casual outfits, not just cowboy looks. The entire belt is knit with just one stitch—the lattice stitch—and uses a double strand of suede yarn to increase stability without making the belt too heavy. Use this countrified accessory to spice up any relaxed look.

SKILL LEVEL
Easy

SIZE
Small (fits up to 28-inch waist), Medium (fits up to 31-inch waist), Large (fits up to 33-inch waist)
Shown in size Medium

FINISHED MEASUREMENTS
Length: 30 (33, 36)"/ 76 (84, 91)cm including buckle
Height: 1¾"/4.4cm

YARN
1 ball of Berroco Suede Deluxe (85% nylon/10% rayon/5% polyester, 1.75oz/50g = approx 100 yd/92m per ball) in #3901 Dale Evans Gold OR approx 100 yd/ 92m nylon/rayon/polyester blend, medium-weight yarn

MATERIALS
• Size 9 U.S.(5.5mm) needles or size to obtain gauge
• 1 Tandy Leather Factory Silvery Floral Buckle Set #1872-01 in gold and silver plate OR 1 1"/(2.5cm) buckle set with keeper
• Tapestry needle
• Spray starch (optional)

GAUGE
8 sts = 2"/5cm over St st using double strand of yarn
Always take time to check your gauge.

PATTERN NOTES
• Unwind half the ball of yarn, cut yarn. Use 2 strands of yarn held together to knit the belt. After working the Lattice Stitch pattern, work the Decrease Rows and the buckle hole.
• Both chart and written instructions for Lattice Stitch pattern are provided. Choose the instruction method you prefer.
• The chart begins with a WS row. If using chart, take care to work WS rows (including Row 1) from left to right, and RS rows from right to left.
• Instructions are given for size S, with sizes (M, L) in parentheses. When only one number is given, it pertains to all sizes. Take care to follow the set of instructions that pertains to your chosen size throughout.

SPECIAL ABBREVIATIONS
K2tog: Knit 2 together
Tbl: Through back loop
LT: With RH needle behind LH needle, skip the first st and k second st tbl, insert RH needle into backs of both sts, k2tog tbl.
RT: K2tog, leaving both sts on needle; insert RH needle between 2 sts, and k first st again; then slip both sts from needle.
St st: Knit RS rows, purl WS rows

STITCH PATTERN
Lattice Stitch (over 8 sts)
Row 1 and all WS rows: Purl
Row 2 (RS): LT, k2, LT, RT
Row 4: K1, LT, k2, RT, k1
Row 6: RT, LT, RT, k2
Row 8: K3, LT, k3
Rep Rows 1–8 for Lattice St patt.

BELT
Unwind half the ball, cut yarn. Holding 2 strands of yarn together, cast on 8 stitches. Work in Lattice St patt until piece measures 28(31, 34)"/71(78.7, 86.4)cm, ending with a RS row.

Decrease Rows
Row 1 (WS): P1, p2tog, p2, p2tog, p1 (6 sts remain)
Row 2: Knit across
Row 3: P2, p2tog, p2 (5 sts remain)
Row 4: Knit
Row 5: Purl
Work in St st until piece measures 1¾"/4.4cm from Dec Row 1, ending with a WS row.

Buckle Hole
Row 1 (RS): K1, k2tog, yo, k2.
Row 2 (WS): Purl across
Row 3: Knit
Row 4: Purl
Work in St st until piece measures 2"/5cm from Row 1 of buckle hole. Bind off all 5 sts.

STITCH CHART
(Lattice Stitch) (over 8 sts)

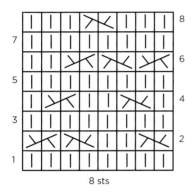

8 sts

Rep Rows 1–8

Legend

Knit on RS, Purl on WS

Left twist

Right twist

ATACHING KEEPER AND BUCKLE

- With RS of belt facing, slip shaped end of belt through the Keeper until Keeper rests on Decrease Row 3.
- Slip the buckle under the shaped end of the belt, poking the prong up through the yo hole. Slip shaped end of belt downward through the buckle. Fold the shaped end backward under the buckle and along underside of belt to the Keeper and stitch in place. Stitch sides of doubled belt end together, working over Keeper.

POINTED EDGE OF BELT

Fold one corner of cast-on edge over to WS, stitch in place. Repeat for other edge, forming a pointed edge.

FINISHING

Weave in ends. Block. If desired, apply spray starch to the back of the belt, following directions on the can. Air-dry.

DESIGN TIP

Many buckles come with a tip that can be easily added at the pointed end of the belt.

LACY WAVE BELT

Going for a hipster rather than the traditional belt? Try this lacy waist cincher—a step upward for any beginner who wants to go beyond knit and purl. With its simple yarn overs, you will find this belt easy to accomplish and delightfully feminine.

SKILL LEVEL
Easy

SIZE
Small (fits up to 28-inch waist), Medium (fits up to 30-inch waist), Large (fits up to 34-inch waist), Extra Large (fits up to 36-inch waist)
Shown in size Medium

FINISHED MEASUREMENTS
Length: 30 (32, 36, 38)"/76.2 (81, 91, 96.5cm) with buckle fastened
Height: 3½"/8.9cm

YARN
1 ball of Berroco Suede (100% nylon, 1.75oz/50g = approx 120 yd/110m per ball) in #3792 Chickadee Pink OR approx 120 yd/110m nylon, medium-weight ribbon yarn in light pink

MATERIALS
• Size 8 U.S. (5mm) needles OR size to obtain gauge
• 1 MJ Trimmings 1½"/3.8cm gold bottle opener buckle #28813 OR 1½"/3.8cm bottle opener buckle in gold
• Tapestry needle for weaving in ends and attaching the buckle
• Spray starch (optional)

GAUGE
19 sts and 28 rows = 4"/10cm over St st

Always take time to check your gauge.

PATTERN NOTES
• Both chart and written instructions for Wave Lace Stitch patt are provided. Choose the instruction method you prefer.
• The chart begins with a WS row. If using chart, take care to work WS rows (including Row 1) from left to right, and RS rows from right to left.
• Instructions are given for size S, with sizes (M, L, XL) in parentheses. When only one number is given, it pertains to all sizes. Take care to follow the set of instructions that pertains to your chosen size throughout.

SPECIAL ABBREVIATIONS
Inc 1: Knit into front, then into back of stitch.
K2tog: Knit 2 stitches together.
K3tog: Knit 3 stitches together
Skp: Slip 1 stitch, knit next stitch. Pass the slipped stitch over the knit stitch and off the needle.
St st: Stockinette stitch
Yo: Yarn over

STITCH PATTERN
Wave Lace Stitch (over 18 sts, inc to 20 sts, dec back to 18 sts)
Begin with 18 sts.
Row 1 and all WS rows: K2, (p2, yo, k2tog, k1), purl to last 2 sts, k2.
Row 2 (RS): K2, yo, Skp, yo, k5, yo, k3, (p2, yo, k2tog), k2. (20 sts)
Row 4: K1, [Skp, yo] twice, k2, k3tog, k4, (p2, yo, k2tog), k2. (18 sts)
Row 6: K1, [Skp, yo] twice, k2, k2tog, k3, (p2, yo, k2tog), k2. (17 sts)
Row 8: K1, [Skp, yo] twice, k2, k2tog, k2, (p2, yo, k2tog), k2. (16 sts)
Row 10: K1, [Skp, yo] twice, k2, k2tog, k1, (p2, yo, k2tog), k2. (15 sts)
Row 12: K2, (yo, Skp, yo), k1, yo, k2, k2tog, (p2, yo, k2tog), k2. (16 sts)
Row 14: K2, (yo, Skp, yo), k3, yo, k3, (p2, yo, k2tog), k2. (18 sts)
Rep Rows 1–14 for Wave Lace Stitch patt.

BELT
Cast on 8 sts.
Row 1 (RS): Inc 1, knit to last st, inc 1. (10 sts)
Row 2 (WS): Inc 1, purl to last st, inc 1. (12 sts)
Rep Rows 1 and 2 until there are 18 sts, ending with a Row 1. Begin Wave Lace St patt. Rep Rows 1–14 13 (14, 16, 17) times total, then work Rows 1–9 once more. Belt should measure approx 28 (30, 34, 36)"/71 (76, 86, 91) cm from beg.

STITCH CHART
(Wave Lace Stitch) (over 18 sts, increase to 20 sts, decrease back to 18 sts)

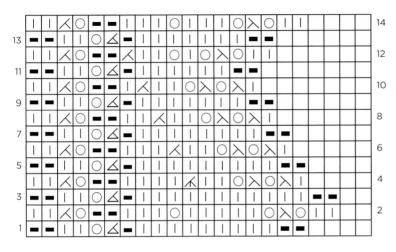

Rep Rows 1–14

Legend

I	Knit on RS, Purl on WS
▬	Purl on RS, Knit on WS
O	Yarn over
⟋	K2tog on WS
⟍	Skp
⟋	K2tog
⋏	K3tog
	No stitch

Next row (RS): Skp, knit across to last 2 sts, k2tog. (14 sts)

Next row (WS): Skp, purl across to last 2 sts, p2tog. (12 sts)

Rep last 2 rows once more. (8 sts remain)

Bind off all 8 sts.

FINISHING
If desired, apply spray starch to back of belt following direction on can. Looking at the back of the buckles and noting the right and left sides, place right buckle on the bound-off end of the belt. Slip bound-off end of belt through right buckle, then turn end downward along WS of belt up to the Wave Lace st patt. Stitch in place. Repeat for the left side. Weave in ends.

DESIGN TIP
Instead of using a buckle, use leftover yarn for a front tie.

FLOWER PIN

This felted brooch adds a fanciful touch to any outfit and can be worn on jackets, hats, belts, purses, shirts, tops, and sweaters. The flower itself requires only simple techniques—felting the knitted fabric, cutting out the petals, and sewing them together—and even a beginning knitter will find it a snap to make. A touch of beading along the edges provides sparkle, texture, and dimension.

SKILL LEVEL
Beginner

SIZE
One size

FINISHED MEASUREMENTS
Diameter 3½"/9cm, felted

YARN
1 skein of Brown Sheep Nature Spun (100% wool yarn, 3.5 oz/100g = approx 245 yd/ 224m per skein) in color #N99 OR approx 245 yd/224m wool, worsted weight
yarn in pink

MATERIALS
- Size 7 U.S. (4.5mm) needles or size to obtain gauge
- Scissors
- 1 tube of Blue Moons Beads Premium Czech Seed Beads in #51665 purple OR 196 glass seed beads in purple
- Tapestry needle
- Sewing needle
- Matching thread
- 1 package Westrim Crafts Pin Back/Self-Adhesive #5868/4 (1.5"/3.8cm 20 pcs) OR 1½"/3.8cm self-adhesive pin back

GAUGE
20 sts = 4"/10cm over St st
Always take time to check your gauge.

FLOWER PIN
Cast on 55 stitches. *Knit 1 row, purl 1 row; rep from * until piece measures 9"/23cm from beginning.

FELTING
Follow the instructions for felting on page 39. Air dry the rectangular fabric.

CUTTING THE PETALS AND STAMEN
Using the templates (see page 56), cut 5 big petals, 4 small petals, and 1 stamen.

ARRANGING THE PETALS
Arrange the petals as follows: Overlap the 5 big petals in a circle, and stitch into place. Overlap the 4 small petals in a circle, stitch into place. Place the set of small petals on top of the big petals and stitch together in the center. Curl up the stamen and stitch into place at center of WS of lower edge.

ATTACHING THE BEADS
String sewing thread with beads. Sew 20 beads along edges of each petal as shown in photo. Sew 16 beads in a swirl design along the stamen as shown.

FINISHING
Fasten pin to the back of the flower.

DESIGN TIP
This project is great for leftover yarns. You can knit several different yarn strands together for an amazing multi-color look when felted. Just be sure to choose only 100% wool yarn, as synthetics will not felt.

TEMPLATES FOR
PETALS AND STAMEN
(Actual size—photocopy at 100%)

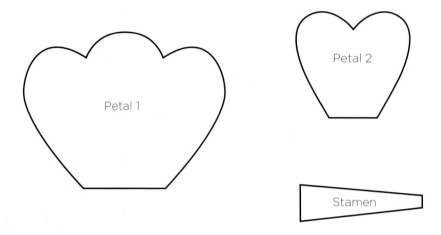

Petal 1

Petal 2

Stamen

DEWDROP LACE SCARF

Romantic, feminine, and soft—these are just some of the words to describe this warm cashmere scarf, which makes a lovely accent to coats and jackets. Its lace rib stitch and simple lace pattern are well suited to the advanced beginner's skills. It looks harder to make than it is, and makes a beautiful gift that will impress.

SKILL LEVEL
Easy

SIZE
One size fits most

FINISHED MEASUREMENTS
4" x 39"/10 x 99cm, including edging, after blocking

YARN
1 ball of Filatura Di Crosa/Tahki Stacy Charles, Inc. Elen Cashmere (25% cashmere/35% extra fine wool/5% silk/35% viscose, 50g = approx 148 yd/135.3m per ball) in color # 01 Pastel Blue or approx 148 yd/135.3m cashmere/wool/silk/rayon blend, lightweight yarn in pastel blue

MATERIALS
• Size 6 U.S. (4mm) needles or size to obtain gauge
• Tapestry needle

GAUGE
22 sts = 4"/10cm over St st
Always take time to check your gauge.

PATTERN NOTES
• Throughout pattern, keep first and last 2 sts of each row in Seed St for border.
• Both chart and written instructions for Dew Drop Lace Stitch patt are provided. Choose the instruction method you prefer.

• For instructions on working I-cord, see page 32.

SPECIAL ABBREVIATIONS
Skp: Slip one stitch, knit next stitch. Pass the slipped stitch over the knit stitch and off the needle.
K2tog: Knit two stitches together.
Yo: Yarn over

STITCH PATTERNS
Dew Drop Lace Stitch (over a multiple of 5 sts plus 1 extra)
Row 1 (RS): K1, *k2tog, yo, k1, yo, Skp, rep from * to end.
Rep 2 (WS): Purl
Rep Rows 1–2 for Dew Drop Lace St patt.

Rib Stitch (over a multiple of 5 sts plus 1 extra)
Row 1 (RS): P1, *k1, sl 1, k1, p2; rep from * to end.
Row 2 (WS): *K2, p3; rep from * to last st, k1.
Rep Rows 1–2 for Rib St patt.

Seed Stitch
Row 1 (RS): *K1, p1; rep from * across.
Row 2: Purl the knit sts and knit the purl sts.

SCARF
Cast on 25 stitches. Work two rows in Seed St. Begin Dewdrop Lace St patt over center 21 sts, keeping first 2 and last 2 sts in Seed St throughout. *Repeat Dewdrop Lace St patt 10 times (20 rows), ending with a WS row. On RS, work Rib St patt over center 21 sts for 20 rows, maintaining Seed St edges, ending with a WS row. Repeat from * 3 more times. Work Dewdrop Lace St patt over center 21 sts as before for 20 rows more. Work one row in Seed St. Bind off in Seed St.

FINISHING
Block scarf to measurements.

I-CORD EDGING
Attaching Cord
Cast on 2 sts, leaving a 2"/5cm tail. Work in I-cord for 7 rows. Slip 2 sts onto stitch holder. Take end of 2"/5cm tail and, RS facing, pull through edge of one narrow end of scarf at corner, securing tightly to edge of scarf.

First Level
*[Slip 2 sts back onto needle, then with second needle, slip second st over the first st and off the needle, leaving 1 st on needle. Slip tip of same needle into the edge of scarf 1/2"/1.27cm from previous attachment of I-cord. Pick up and knit 1 stitch (2 sts on ndl). Work in I-cord for 7 rows]; rep from * 6 more times, making sure each loop is spaced 1/2"/1.27cm apart. (7 loops created).

STITCH CHART
(Dew Drop Lace Stitch)
(over a multiple of 5 sts plus 1 extra)

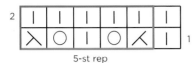

Rep Rows 1–2

5-st rep

Legend

I	Knit on RS, Purl on WS
λ	K2tog
O	Yarn over
λ	Skp

Second Level

Work as directed in Attaching Cord but begin by attaching to center of first loop. Rep from * of First Level 6 times total, picking up st through center of I-cord loop instead of edge of scarf. (6 loops created) Weave in loose ends.
Repeat both levels of I-cord edging for opposite narrow end of scarf.

DESIGN TIP

Add beads to the scarf for a glamorous look. When making the I-cord edging, slip a bead with a large hole through t he I-cord before attaching loop to the edge of scarf.

ENTWINED CABLE SCARF

Make a bold statement with flowing cables, knit in rich alpaca-blend yarn. This smart scarf sports a classic fringed design that will polish your look, complementing winter coats and jackets. It's a stylish look for people on the go that works with business as well as casual attire, and can be worn by both men and women.

SKILL LEVEL
Easy

SIZE
One size fits most

FINISHED MEASUREMENTS
6" x 46"/15 x 117cm, blocked

YARN
1 hank of Berroco Ultra Alpaca (50% alpaca/50% wool, 3.5 oz/100g = approx 215 yd/197m per hank) in color # 6249 Fennel OR approx 215 yd/197m alpaca/wool blend, medium-weight yarn

MATERIALS
• Size 8 U.S. (5mm) needles or size to obtain gauge
• Tapestry needle
• Cable needle
• Crochet hook
• 4"/10cm-wide cardboard strip for making the fringe

GAUGE
20 sts and 26 rows = 4"/10cm over St st
Always take time to check your gauge.

PATTERN NOTES
• The Entwined Cable Stitch patt will be worked twice on each side. Rib will be worked in the center.
• Throughout, keep first and last 2 stitches of each row in Seed St for border. These 2 stitches at each edge are not included in chart.
• Both chart and written instructions for Entwined Cable Stitch patt are provided. Choose the instruction method you prefer.

SPECIAL ABBREVIATIONS
7-st Right Purl Cable: Slip 4 sts to cable needle and hold to back of work, k3, slip first (purl) st on cable needle back to LH needle, p1 from LH needle, then k3 from cable needle.

7-st Left Purl Cable: Slip 4 sts to cable needle and hold to front of work, k3, slip first (purl) st on cable needle back to LH needle, p1 from LH needle, then k3 from cable needle.

STITCH PATTERN
Entwined Cable Stitch
(over 31 sts)
Rows 1 and 17 (RS): [K3, p1] 3 times, 7-st Right Purl Cable, [p1, k3] 3 times.
Row 2 and all WS rows: K the knit sts and p the purl sts
Rows 3, 7, 11, 15, 19, 21, 23, 27, 29, 31; K the knit sts and p the purl sts.
Rows 5 and 13: [K3, p1] twice, [7-st Left Purl Cable, p1] twice, k3, p1, k3.

Row 9: K3, [p1, 7-st Right Purl Cable] 3 times, p1, k3.
Row 25: 7-st Right Purl Cable, [p1, k3] 4 times, p1, 7-st Left Purl Cable.
Row 32: Rep Row 2.
Rep Rows 1–32 twice for Entwined Cable St patt,

Rib Stitch
(over 31 sts)
Row 1 (RS): *K3, p1; rep from * 7 times, end k3.
Row 2 (WS): *P3, k1; rep from * 7 times, end p3.
Rep Rows 1–2 for Rib St.

Seed Stitch
Row 1 (RS): *K1, p1; rep from * across.
Row 2: Purl the knit sts and knit the purl sts.

SCARF
Cast on 35 stitches. Work Rib Stitch over center 31 sts for 12 rows, keeping 2 sts at beg and end of each row in Seed St. Begin Entwined Cable St patt over center 31 sts, maintaining edge sts in Seed St, working Rows 1–32 twice. Work Rib Stitch over center 31 sts as before, maintaining edge sts in Seed St, until scarf measures 34"/86.4 cm from beg, ending with a WS row. Work Entwined Cable St patt over center 31 sts, maintaining edge sts in Seed St, working rows 1–32 twice more. Bind off all sts.

STITCH CHART
(Entwined Cable Stitch)
(over 31 sts)

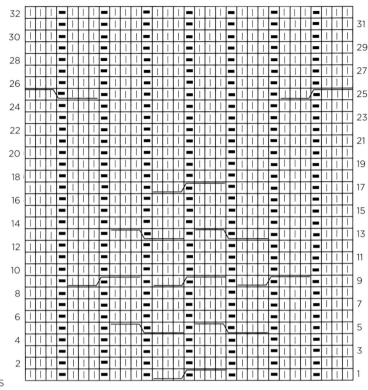

Legend

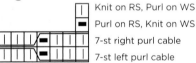

| Knit on RS, Purl on WS
| Purl on RS, Knit on WS
7-st right purl cable
7-st left purl cable

FRINGE

Make 34. The general instructions for making fringe are on page 37. Wrap the yarn once around the width of the cardboard strip. For each edge, use crochet hook to attach 17 fringes to each narrow end of scarf, evenly spaced along edge. Trim ends evenly.

FINISHING

Weave in ends.

DESIGN TIP

You can turn this into an allover cable scarf by working only the Entwined Cable pattern over the center 31 stitches throughout.

MOEBIUS SHAWL

With a simple easy twist and no shaping, our delicate, watercolor Moebius shawl keeps you warm while looking hip. This versatile piece can also be worn as a head and neck wrap, and its simple reversible lace stitch will match any beginning knitter's skills. Mastering this stitch is easy—and leads to a fashion accessory that is both lovely and eyecatching.

SKILL LEVEL
Beginner

SIZE
One size

FINISHED MEASUREMENTS
16" x 45"/40.5 x 114cm

YARN
1 hank Colinette/Unique Kolours Lasso (100% nylon, 3.5oz/100g = approx 210 yd/192m per hank) in #127 Morocco OR approx 220 yd/201m nylon, worsted weight yarn

MATERIALS
- Size 8 U.S. (5mm) needles or size to obtain gauge
- Tapestry needle

GAUGE
12 sts = 4"/10cm over Faggoting St
Always take time to check your gauge.

PATTERN NOTE
One edge of the shawl will be twisted once and sewn to the other edge of the shawl, creating a Mobius look. The Faggoting St pattern is reversible.

SPECIAL ABBREVIATIONS
K2tog: Knit two stitches together.
Yo: Yarn over

STITCH PATTERN
Faggoting Stitch
(over a multiple of 2 sts plus 3 extra)
Row 1: K2, *yo, k2tog; rep from * to last st, k1.
Rep Row 1 for Faggoting St.

SHAWL
Cast on 49 stitches. Work Faggoting St patt until piece measures 45"/114.3cm from beg. Bind off all 49 stitches.

TWISTING THE SHAWL
Lay shawl on surface. Flip one end of shawl over to reverse side, creating a twist in the shawl at that end. Whipstitch side edges together without removing the twist, creating a crossover look.

FINISHING
Weave in ends.

DESIGN TIP
If you are in a rush for a last-minute gift, this is the project to make.

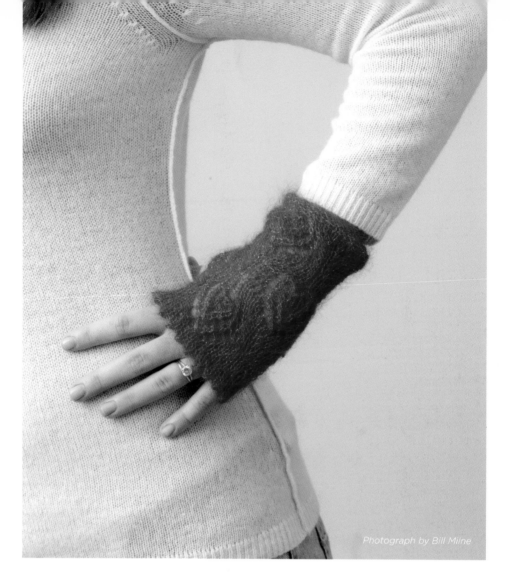

Photograph by Bill Milne

FINGERLESS GLOVES

Treat your hard-knitting hands to the soft touch of mohair. These stylish fingerless gloves are made with lace stitches that reveal specks of gold sparkle. Suitable for day or evening wear, they keep your hands warm while leaving your fingers free for handling keys, bus fare, buttons, zippers—or anything else you need to get a grip on.

SKILL LEVEL
Intermediate

SIZE
One size fits most

FINISHED MEASUREMENTS
Circumference: 7"/17.8cm (stretchable)
Length: 6½"/16.5cm

YARN
1 ball of Rowan Kidsilk Night (67% super kid mohair/18% silk/10% polyester/5% nylon, 0.9oz/25g = approx 227 yd/208m per ball) in #609 Dazzle OR approx 227 yd/208m mohair/silk/polyester/nylon blend, worsted weight yarn

MATERIALS
• Size 6 U.S. (4mm) needles or size to obtain gauge
• Tapestry needle for seaming and weaving in ends
• Stitch markers

GAUGE
22 sts = 4"/10cm over St st
Always take time to check your gauge.

PATTERN NOTES
• The picot edging will be turned to WS at its midpoint, forming picots, and whip-stitched down on the inside of gloves.
• Both chart and written instructions for Leaf Lace Stitch (Chart A) and Rib Stitch (Chart B) are provided. Choose the instruction method you prefer.
• Charts A and B begin with a WS row. If using charts, take care to work WS rows (including Row 1) from left to right, and RS rows from right to left.

SPECIAL ABBREVIATIONS
Skp: Slip 1 stitch, knit next stitch. Pass the slipped stitch over the knit stitch and off the needle.
S2kp: Slip 2 stitches, knit next stitch. Pass the 2 slipped stitches over the knit st and off the needle.
K2tog: Knit 2 stitches together.
K3tog: Knit 3 stitches together.
K1tbl: Knit 1 st though the back loop.
Inc 9: (Knit in front and back of next stitch) 9 times.
Pm: Place marker
Yo: Yarn over

STITCH PATTERNS
Leaf Lace Stitch
Begin with 27 sts.
Row 1 and all WS rows: Purl across.
Row 2 (RS): K2, [yo, Skp] twice, k5, [k2tog, yo] twice, k2, Skp, k1, k2tog, k5. (25 sts)
Row 4: K3, [yo, Skp] twice, k3, [k2tog, yo] twice, k2, Skp, k1, k2tog, k4. (23 sts)
Row 6: K4, [yo, Skp] twice, k1, [k2tog, yo] twice, k2, Skp, k1, k2tog, k3. (21 sts)
Row 8: K5, yo, Skp, yo, S2kp, yo, k2tog, yo, k2, Skp, k1, k2tog, k2. (19 sts)
Row 10: K6, yo, Skp, k1, k2tog, yo, k8. (19 sts)
Row 12: K7, yo, S2kp, yo, k9. (19 sts)
Row 14: K15, Inc 9, k3. (27 sts)
Row 16: K5, Skp, k1, k2tog, k2, [yo, Skp] twice, k5, [k2tog, yo] twice, k2. (25 sts)
Row 18: K4, Skp, k1, k2tog, k2, [yo, Skp] twice, k3, [k2tog, yo] twice, k3. (23 sts)
Row 20: K3, Skp, k1, k2tog, k2, [yo, Skp] twice, k1, [k2tog, yo] twice, k4. (21 sts)
Row 22: K2, Skp, k1, k2tog, k2, yo, Skp, yo, S2kp, yo, k2tog, yo, k5. (19 sts)
Row 24: K8, yo, Skp, k1, k2tog, yo, k6. (19 sts)
Row 26: K9, yo, S2kp, yo, k7. (19 sts)
Row 28: K3, Inc 9, k15. (27 sts)
Work rows 1–28 once, then Rows 1–12 once more for Leaf Lace St patt.

Rib Stitch
(over a multiple of 3 sts plus 2 extra)
Row 1 (WS): Knit
Row 2 (RS): P2, *k1tbl, p2; rep from * across.
Rep Rows 1–2 for Rib St patt.

STITCH CHARTS

CHART A
(Leaf Lace Stitch)
(begins with 27 sts)

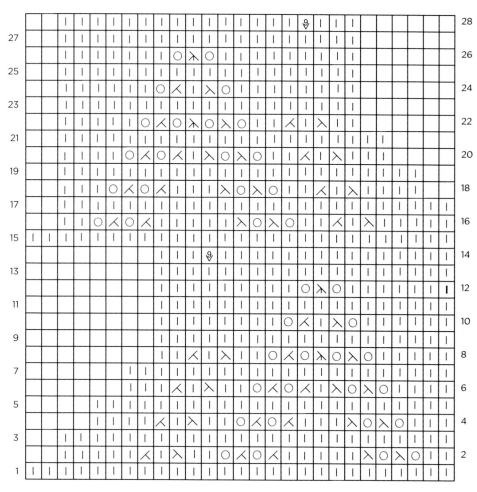

Legend

I	Knit on RS, Purl on WS
O	Yarn over
⅄	Skp
⅄	K2tog
⅄	S2kp
ϑ	Inc 9
	No stitch

CHART B
(Rib Stitch)
(over a multiple of 3 sts plus 2 extra)

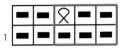

2

Rep Rows 1-2

1

3-st rep

Legend

▬	Knit on WS, Purl on RS
⚇	Knit st through back loop (K1tbl)

Picot Edging
Rows 1 and 3 (WS):
Purl across.
Rows 2 and 4 (RS):
Knit across.
Row 5: K1, *yo, k2tog; rep from
* across, end with yo, k3tog.
Row 6: Knit
Row 7: Purl
Row 8: Knit
Bind off loosely.

GLOVES
Right Glove
Cast on 46 sts.
Work 14 sts in Rib St, pm, work
27 sts in Leaf Lace St, pm,
work 5 sts in Rib St. Continuing in patts, keeping first 14 sts
and last 5 sts in Rib St, work
Rows 1–28 of Leaf Lace St over
27 sts once, then work Rows
1–12 of Leaf Lace St over these
sts once more, ending with
a RS row. Work Picot Edging
over all sts.

Left Glove
Cast on 46 sts.
Work 5 sts in Rib St, pm, work
27 sts in Leaf Lace St, pm,
work 14 sts in Rib St. Continuing in patts, keeping first 5 sts
and last 14 sts in Rib St, work
Rows 1–28 of Leaf Lace St over
27 sts once, then work Rows
1–12 of Leaf Lace St over these
sts once more, ending with
a RS row. Work Picot Edging
over all sts.

HEM
Fold the Picot Edging at midpoint and turn down to WS.
Whipstitch the picot hem on
WS of work, making sure the
picot is visible over edge
of glove.

FINISHING
With RS facing, for each glove
sew bottom 3"/7.6cm of side
edges together, beg at cast-
on edge of glove. Beg at Picot
Edge, sew top 1¼"/3.2cm of
upper side edges together
There will be a 2¼"/5.7cm
gap between the two seams—
leave this open for the thumb.
Weave in ends.

DESIGN TIP
You can convert your gloves
into arm warmers by making
them longer before working
the picot edging.

FELTED CLOCHE

Fold up your hat brim, add the simple knitted flower, and ooh-la-la—
a sophisticated new look to frame your face! This felted hat is super-
simple, with basic stitches and fun-to-do felting techniques. Best of all,
it looks great on women of every age!

SKILL LEVEL
Easy

SIZE
One size fits most (21 to 22½"/52.5 to 56cm head circumference)

FINISHED MEASUREMENTS
Hat circumference: 21 to 22½"/52.5 to 56cm head circumference
Flower diameter: 4½"/11.4cm

YARN
1 ball of Brown Sheep Nature Spun (100% wool yarn, 3.5 oz/100g = approx 245 yd/224m per ball) in color #N40 Grape Harvest OR approx 245 yd/224m wool, medium-weight yarn.

MATERIALS
- Size 7 U.S. (4.5mm) double-pointed and 16" circular needle or size to obtain gauge
- Tapestry needle
- Scissors
- 1 tube of Blue Moons Beads Premium Czech Seed Beads #51665 in purple OR 40 glass seed beads
- Sewing needle and
- Matching thread

GAUGE
20 sts = 4"/10cm over St st
Always take time to check your gauge.

PATTERN NOTE
The entire hat is knitted in the round. Begin with double-pointed needles, changing to circular needle when hat becomes larger. Knitting begins at the crown (top) of hat, followed by the body and then the brim.

SPECIAL ABBREVIATIONS
Rnd: Round
Inc 1: Increase by knitting into front, then into the back of the same stitch
Dpn: Double-pointed needles

HAT
Crown
Cast on 12 stitches. Divide evenly on 3 dpns so that each needle holds 4 sts. Place marker at beg of round.
Rnd 1 and all odd-numbered rounds: Knit 1 round.
Rnd 2: *K1, inc 1; rep from * across. (18 sts)
Rnd 4: Rep rnd 2. (27 sts)
Rnd 6: *(K1, inc 1) 4 times, k1; rep from * twice more. (39 sts)
Rnd 8: *(K1, inc 1) 6 times, k1; rep from * twice more. (57 sts)
Rnd 10: *(Inc 1, k2) 6 times, inc 1; rep from * twice more. (76 sts)

Body
Rnd 1: (Inc 1, k37) twice. (78 sts)
Rnd 2: (Inc 1, k38) twice. (80 sts)
Rnd 3: (Inc 1, k39) twice. (82 sts)
Rnd 4: (Inc 1, k40) twice. (84 sts)
Rnd 5: (Inc 1, k41) twice. (86 sts)
Rnd 6: (Inc 1, k42) twice. (88 sts)
Rnd 7: (Inc 1, k43) twice. (90 sts)

Knit every round for 6"/15 cm.

Next rnd: *(Inc 1, k14); rep from * across. (96 sts)
Next rnd: Knit across
Next rnd: *(Inc 1, k15); rep from * across. (102 sts)
Next rnd: Knit across
Next rnd: *(Inc 1, k16); rep from * across. (108 sts)
Next rnd: Knit across
Next rnd: *(Inc 1, k17); rep from * across. (114 sts)
Next rnd: Knit across
Next rnd: *(Inc 1, k18); rep from * across. (120 sts)

Brim
*(Knit one round, purl next round); rep from * 4 times more (10 rounds total). Bind off.

FLOWER TEMPLATE FOR PETALS AND BEAD PLACEMENT

(Actual size—photocopy at 100%)

Cut out 4 Large, 4 Medium, and 4 Small petals from felted fabric. Sew 2 Large petals together at their flat edges; repeat for remaining Large, Medium and Small petals. There will be 6 two-ended petals. *Place Large petal on a table, place second Large petal on top of it forming an X, and stitch in place. Repeat for remaining Medium and Small petals. There will be 1 stack each of Large, Medium, and Small flowers. Place Medium flowers on top of Large flowers. Stitch in place. Place Small flowers on top of Medium flowers. Stitch in place. Sew three beads on each corner of petals. Sew four beads in the center.

O = bead placement

Large Petal

Medium Petal

small Petal

FELTING

The general instructions for felting are on page 39. It generally takes about 7–12 minutes to felt the hat. Check hat frequently during felting and stop the process when desired result is achieved. Do not allow the hat to dry before moving on to Shaping the Hat.

SHAPING

Stretch out the crown, the body, and the brim of the hat to fit as desired. You can place the hat on your head as needed to check fit.

FINISHING HAT

After stretching, air-dry the hat to retain the shape. You can place the felted hat on an upside-down bowl, a blown–up balloon, a hat form, or any type of rounded edge that will support the hat's shape.

FELTED FLOWER

Cast on 45 stitches. *(Knit one row, purl one row); rep from * until piece measures 5 1/2"/14cm. Bind off. Felt piece as instructed on page 39.

ATTACHING FLOWER TO HAT

Upturn one side of brim. Stitch flower in place through brim into hat.

DESIGN TIP

If you prefer, instead of sewing the flower to the cloche, add a pin backing to the flower so that it can be used as a brooch.

CABLED LEGWARMERS WITH ARMWARMER VARIATION

These elegantly styled mini-legwarmers put a modern spin on an eighties flashback. Cables and ribs intricately twine upward, creating a warm woolly look that will dress up any outfit while keeping legs fashionably cozy even in the iciest winds. The armwarmer variation features a simple thumb hook.

SKILL LEVEL
Easy

SIZE
One size fits most

FINISHED MEASUREMENTS
Width: 7¹/2"/19.1cm
Height: 11¹/2"/29.2cm

YARN
1 skein of Brown Sheep Nature Spun (100% wool yarn, 3.5 oz/ 100g = approx 245 yd/224m per skein) in #522 Nervous Green OR approx 245 yd/224m wool, medium-weight yarn in green

MATERIALS
- Size 4 and 7 U.S. (3.5 and 4.5mm) needles or size to obtain gauge
- Cable needle
- Tapestry needle for seaming and weaving in ends

GAUGE
20 sts = 4"/10cm over St st using larger needle
Always take time to check your gauge.

PATTERN NOTES
- The legwarmer begins with an Arctic Cable pattern worked once, followed by a repeated Rib Stitch pattern. Arm warmer version is also provided.
- Both chart and written instructions for Arctic Cable patt are provided. Choose the instruction method you prefer.

SPECIAL ABBREVIATIONS
4-st Right Cable: Slip 2 sts to cable needle and hold to back of work, k2, k2 from cable needle.
4-st Left Cable: Slip 2 sts to cable needle and hold to front of work, k2, k2 from cable needle.
4-st Right Twist: Slip 2 sts to cable needle and hold to back of work, k2, p2 from cable needle.
4-st Left Twist: Slip 2 sts to cable needle and hold to front of work, p2, k2 from cable needle.

STITCH PATTERNS
Arctic Cable
(over a multiple of 32 sts plus 2 extra)
Row 1 (RS): *P2, k2; rep from * to last two sts, p2.
Row 2 and all WS rows: K the knit sts, p the purl sts.
Row 3: *(P2, k2) 3 times, 4-st Right Cable, p2, 4-st Left Cable, (k2, p2) twice, k2; rep from * once more, p2.
Row 5: *(P2, k2) twice, p2, 4-st Right Twist, k2, p2, k2, 4-st Left Twist, (p2, k2) twice; rep from * once more, p2.
Row 7: *(P2, k2) twice, 4-st Right Cable, (p2, k2) twice, p2, 4-st Left Cable, k2, p2, k2; rep from * once more, p2.

Row 9: *P2, k2, p2, 4-st Right Twist, (k2, p2) 3 times, k2, 4-st Left Twist, p2, k2; rep from * once more, p2.
Row 11: *P2, k2, 4-st Right Cable, (p2, k2) 4 times, p2, 4-st Left Cable, k2; rep from * once more, p2.
Row 13: *P2, 4-st Right Twist, k2, p2, k2, 4-st Right Cable, p2, 4-st Left Cable, k2, p2, k2, 4-st Left Twist; rep from * once more, p2.
Row 15: Rep Row 5.
Row 17: Rep Row 7.
Row 19: Rep Row 9.
Row 21: Rep Row 1.
Row 23: Rep Row 3.
Row 25: Rep Row 5.
Row 27: Rep Row 1.
Row 29: *(P2, k2) twice, p2, 4-st Left Cable, k2, p2, k2, 4-st Right Cable, (p2, k2) twice; rep from * once more, p2.
Row 31: *(P2, k2) 3 times, 4-st Left Twist, p2, 4-st Right Twist, (k2, p2) twice, k2; rep from * once more, p2.
Row 32: K the knit sts, p the purl sts.
Work Rows 1–32 once for Arctic Cable Stitch patt.

Rib Stitch
(over a multiple of 4 sts plus 2 extra)
Row 1 (RS): *P2, k2; rep from * to last two sts, p2.
Row 2 (WS): K the knit sts, p the purl sts.
Rep Rows 1–2 for Rib Stitch patt.

STITCH CHART
(Arctic Cable)
(over a multiple of 32 sts
plus 2 extra)

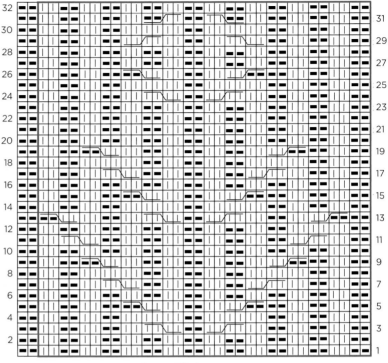

32-st rep

Legend

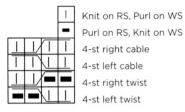

Knit on RS, Purl on WS

Purl on RS, Knit on WS

4-st right cable

4-st left cable

4-st right twist

4-st left twist

LEGWARMER

(Make 2)
Cast on 66 stitches loosely
with smaller needle. Begin
working the Arctic Cable
Stitch pattern for 1½"/3.8cm.
Change to larger needle.
Continue working Arctic Cable
Stitch patt through Row 32,
then work Rib Stitch pattern
over all sts until legwarmer
measures 10"/25cm. Change
to smaller needle. Continue to
work in Rib St patt until legwarmer measures 11½"/29cm.

FINISHING
With RS facing, sew side
edges of legwarmer together.
Weave in ends.

ARMWARMER
VARIATION
Work as for Arctic Legwarmer,
except when sewing seams,
beg at cast-on edge (Cable
section). Sew 1" (2.5cm) seam,
then leave next 2" (5cm) open
for thumb, then sew remainder
of seam.

DESIGN TIP
To make looser legwarmers,
use larger needle throughout.

SCARLET HANDBAG

Stop traffic with a red-hot handbag. The twisted stitch used throughout gives the impression of a light cable, adding a hint of sophistication. Accent it with gold hardware and you have a terrific tote that will complement a variety of looks.

SKILL LEVEL
Intermediate

SIZE
One size

FINISHED MEASUREMENTS
Width: 9¹/₂"/23.75cm
Height: 8"/20cm
Depth: 1¹/₂"/3.75cm

YARN
1 hank of S.R. Kertzer Butterfly Super 10 (100% mercerized cotton yarn, 125g = approx 249 yd/230m per hank) in #3462 OR approx 249 yd/230m mercerized cotton, DK weight yarn

MATERIALS
- Size 6 U.S. (4.0 mm) needles or size to obtain gauge
- ¹/₂ yd (.46m) Heat'n Bond Ultra Hold Iron-On Adhesive OR heavy fusible interfacing
- 2 BagWorks D-Ring Clamp, ³/₄" Gld, Style # A3105-GL OR 2³/₄" D-ring clamp
- 6 27mm split rings, in gold
- 2 MJ Trimming Flat Metal Rings Style #28530 (1"/25mm) in gold OR 2 1"/25mm flat metal rings
- 1 Tandy Leather Company Bag Clasp Closure Style #1300 in gilt finish (1¹/₂" x 1") OR 1¹/₂" x 1" gilt clasp closure
- 2 BagWorks Gold Foot Brad, Style # A3116-GLD in gold OR 2 handbag feet

- ¹/₂ yd (.46m) satin OR lining fabric of your choice
- 2 Sheets 7-mesh plastic canvas
- 12"/30cm of ¹/₂"/1.25cm nylon 3-strand rope
- Tapestry needle
- Matching thread
- Scissors
- Iron
- Straight pins
- Sewing needle

GAUGE
22 sts = 4"/10cm over St st
Always take time to check your gauge.

PATTERN NOTE
Cut out lining for each knitted piece, except handle, before attaching pieces of handbag together. Cut out and fuse Heat'n Bond for each knitted piece, before attaching pieces of handbag together.

SPECIAL ABBREVIATIONS
RT: Right Twist. K2tog, leaving both sts on needle; insert RH needle between 2 sts, and k first st again; then slip both sts from needle.
LT: Left Twist. With RH needle behind LH needle, skip the first st and k second st tbl, insert RH needle into backs of both sts, k2tog tbl.
St st: Stockinette stitch: Knit RS rows, purl WS rows.
K2tog: Knit 2 together.

STITCH PATTERNS
Scarlet Stitch
(over a multiple of 8 sts)
Row 1 (WS): P1, *k2, p2; rep from * to last three sts, k2, p1.
Row 2 (RS): *K1, p1, RT, LT, p1, k1; rep from * to end.
Row 3: *P1, k1, p1, k2, p1, k1, p1; rep from * to end.
Row 4: *K1, RT, p2, LT, k1; rep from * to end.
Row 5: P2, *k4, p4; rep from * to last six sts, k4, p2.
Row 6: Knit across.
Row 7: Repeat Row 5.
Row 8: Repeat Row 6.
Row 9: Repeat Row 1.
Row 10: *LT, p1, k2, p1, RT; rep from * to end.
Row 11: *K1, p1, k1, p2, k1, p1, k1; rep from * to end.
Row 12: *P1, LT, k2, RT, p1; rep from * to end.
Row 13: K2, *p4, k4; rep from * to last six sts, p4, k2.
Row 14: Knit across.
Row 15: Rep Row 13.
Row 16: Rep Row 14.
Rep Rows 1–16 for Scarlet St patt.

Seed Stitch
Row 1 (RS): *K1, p1; rep from * across.
Row 2: Purl the knit sts and knit the purl sts.
Rep Rows 1–2 for Seed St patt

PURSE
Body
(Make 2)
Cast on 56 sts. Begin working the Scarlet St patt for 7"/17.5

cm. Continue in patt, at the same time, dec 1 st at beg and end of every row until 38 sts remain. Bind off all 38 sts on WS.

Flap

Cast on 56 sts. Begin working the Scarlet St patt for 5"/12.5 cm. Continue in patt, at the same time, dec 1 st at beg and end of every row until 38 sts remain. Bind off all 38 sts on WS.

Flap Tab

Cast on 14 sts. Work in Seed St for 4 rows.
Row 5: Work 4 sts, BO 6 sts, work 4 sts in Seed st.
Row 6: Work 4 sts in Seed st, cast on 6 sts, work 4 sts in Seed st.
Work in Seed st for 5 rows. Bind off all sts.

Gusset

Cast on 8 sts. Work in Seed St patt for 24"/60cm. Bind off all sts.

Handle

Cast on 8 sts. Work in Seed St patt for 13"/32.5cm. Bind off all sts.

FINISHING

• On low setting, press knitted pieces on WS.
• Sew tab to bottom center of purse flap.

1. Lay all knitted pieces on Heat 'n Bond, trace and cut.

2. Lay all knitted pieces, except the handle, on lining. Trace, adding an extra 1/2"/1.25cm seam allowance and cut.

3. Place knitted Gusset on plastic canvas. Trace and cut plastic 1/4"/.625cm smaller than Gusset.

4. Fuse sticky surface of Heat 'n Bond on WRONG side of all matching knitted pieces according to manufacturer's directions.

5. With RIGHT sides together, match and sew Gusset's lining to both Body linings' curved edges. (referred to now as Lining)

6. Place and sew plastic canvas on WRONG Side of knitted Gusset.

7. With RIGHT sides together, match and sew knitted Gusset to curved edges of each Body.

8. Find center of one side of Body. Place the clasp of the bag clasp closure in center of knitted piece. Secure in place according to manufacturer's directions. Keep the keyhole aside.

9. Place purse feet on bottom edge of Gusset and through plastic canvas, 6"/15cm apart. Secure into place.

10. With RIGHT sides facing each other, place knitted Body into Lining. Sew top edges together leaving 2"/5cm opening.

11. Turn Lining RIGHT side through 2"/5cm opening. Fold 2"/5cm inward and sew in place.

12. Attach D-ring clamps to either side of Gusset.

13. With RIGHT sides together, match and sew Flap's lining to knitted Flap, leaving a 1"/2.5cm opening.

14. Turn Flap RIGHT side out.

15. Make an incision into the buttonhole, created by the 6-st bind off, on tab through the lining with scissors. Do not worry about basting around the hole. Place keyhole of bag clasp closure in this area. Secure in place according to manufacturer's directions.

STITCH CHART
(Scarlet Stitch)
(over a multiple of 8 sts)

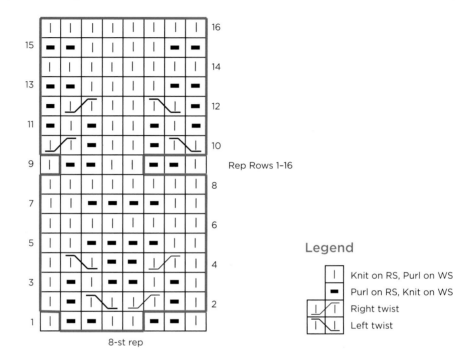

Rep Rows 1–16

8-st rep

Legend

I	Knit on RS, Purl on WS
—	Purl on RS, Knit on WS
╱╱I	Right twist
I╲╲	Left twist

16. Attach bag clasps on Front and Flap together. Overlap 1¹⁄₂"/3.75cm of back edge of Flap over purse back. Center Flap and sew into place with left over yarn strands.

17. Place Handle around 12"/30cm nylon rope. Sew along edge and secure rope into place. Fold both sides around metal rings. Sew side edges into place.

18. Attach three split rings together. Attach one end of the split ring chain to the metal ring on the handle and D-clamp on the purse. Rep for the other side of the handle and D-clamp.

DESIGN TIP
Instead of using Heat 'n Bond to stabilize the bag, you can use fusible felt.

LACE SOCKS

New to sock knitting? Put your best foot forward with a warm
and cozy pair of wool socks dressed up with a pretty lace pattern.
Advanced beginners will find this a challenging but ultimately
an achievable project.

SKILL LEVEL
Easy

SIZE
One size (fits women's shoe sizes 6–8½)

FINISHED MEASUREMENTS
8½"/21.6cm from cuff to heel
8"/20.3cm from heel to toe

YARN
1 skein of Brown Sheep Nature Spun Fingering (100% wool, 1.75oz/50g = approx 310 yd/283.5m per skein) in #N93 Latte OR approx 310 yd/283.5m wool, fingering-weight yarn

MATERIALS
- Size 2 U.S. (2.75mm) double-pointed needles or size to obtain gauge
- Tapestry needle for weaving in ends

GAUGE
28 sts = 4"/10cm over St st
Always take time to check your gauge.

PATTERN NOTES
- You will be knitting in the round with the right side of work facing you, except for Heel and Turn Heel sections.
- When working Petal Lace patt from the chart, read all rounds from right to left.
- The instep sts from the cuff to the heel will be worked in Petal Lace pattern only.
- The instep stitches from the gusset to the toe shaping will be worked in Row 4 only of Petal Lace pattern.
- The toe shaping will all be done in the plain knit st. (*Note:* Since the to shaping will be worked in the round, you will only need to use the knit st.)
- Both chart and written instructions for Petal Lace Pattern are provided. Choose the instruction method you prefer.

SPECIAL ABBREVIATIONS
N1: Needle 1
N2: Needle 2
N3: Needle 3
slp: Slip purlwise
Skp: Slip one stitch, knit next stitch. Pass the slipped stitch over the knit stitch and off the needle.
Sk2p: Slip 1 stitch, knit next 2 stitches together. Pass the slipped stitch over the 2 stitches knit together and off the needle.
Yo: Yarn over
K2tog: Knit 2 stitches together.
Rnd: Round

STITCH PATTERN
Petal Lace Stitch
(over a multiple of 28 sts)
Rnd 1: *[P1, yo, Skp, k1, k2tog, yo, p2, (k1, p1) 3 times]; rep from * once more.
Rnd 2: *[P1, k1, yo, Sk2p, yo, k1, p2, (k1, p1) 3 times]; rep from * once more.
Rnd 3: *[(P1, k1) 3 times, p2, (k1, p1) 3 times]; rep from * once more.
Rnd 4: *[(P1, k1) 3 times, p2, yo, Skp, k1, k2tog, yo, p1]; rep from * once more.
Rnd 5: *[(P1, k1) 3 times, p2, k1, yo, Sk2p, yo, k1, p1]; rep from * once more.
Rnd 6: Repeat Rnd 3
Rnd 7: Repeat Rnd 1.
Rnd 8: Repeat Rnd 2
Rnds 9, 10, and 11: Repeat Rnd 3.
Rnd 12: Repeat Rnd 4.
Rnd 13: Repeat Rnd 5.
Rnd 14: Repeat Rnd 3.
Rep Rounds 1–14 for Petal Lace Stitch patt.

SOCKS
Cuff
Cast on 56 sts loosely. Divide sts over 3 needles as follows:
Needle 1 (N1): 14 sts (heel)
Needle 2 (N2): 28 sts (instep)
Needle 3 (N3): 14 sts (heel)
Place marker and join, taking care not to twist stitches on needles. Slip marker every round.
Round 1: *K1, p1; rep from * around.

Rep Round 1 until 13 rounds are complete. Piece should measure approx 1½"/3.8cm.

Leg
Round 14:
N1: Knit
N2: Begin Petal Lace Stitch patt
N3: Knit
Repeat Round 14 as established, working Petal Lace Stitch pattern over the instep sts on N2 and knitting all heel stitches (N1 and N3) until leg measures approx 6"/15cm from beginning. Then work across stitches on N1 and N2, stopping at N3.

Heel
Slip N3 stitches onto N1. (28 heel sts). With RS facing, begin working back and forth in rows over these 28 sts only as follows:
Row 1 (RS): *Slp 1, k1. Repeat from * to end. Turn.
Row 2 (WS): Slp 1, purl to end.
Repeat Rows 1–2 until 30 heel rows are complete.

Turn Heel
(Worked over 28 sts on N1)
Row 1 (RS): K16, Skp, k1. Turn work.
Row 2 (WS): Slp 1, p5, p2tog, p1. Turn work.
Row 3: Slp 1, k6, Skp, k1. Turn work.
Row 4: Slp 1, p7, p2tog, p1. Turn work.

Row 5: Slp 1, k8, Skp, k1. Turn work.
Row 6: Slp 1, p9, p2tog, p1. Turn work.
Row 7: Slp 1, k10, Skp, k1. Turn work.
Row 8: Slp 1, p11, p2tog, p1. Turn work.
Row 9: Slp 1, k12, Skp, k1. Turn work.
Row 10: Slp 1, p13, p2tog, p1. Turn work.
Row 11: Slp 1, k14, Skp. Turn work.
Row 12: Slp 1, p14, p2tog. Turn work.
Row 13: Knit across first 8 stitches.

Gusset
• With a new needle, knit next 8 stitches. With same needle, pick up and knit 15 stitches along the side edge of the heel. Pick up and knit one st from the row below the first instep stitch to prevent a hole. (24 sts on N1)
• With a free needle, work Row 4 of Petal Lace patt across 28 stitches on Needle 2. (28 sts on N2)
• With free needle, pick up and knit one st from the row below the first heel st to prevent a hole. Pick up and knit 15 stitches along the side edge of the heel, then with same needle, knit the next 8 heel stitches. (24 sts on N3)

Gusset Shaping
Round 1:
N1: Knit to last 3 sts, k2tog, k1.
N2: Knit the knit sts, purl the purl sts.
N3: K1, Skp, knit to the end.
Round 2:
N1: Knit.
N2: Knit the knit sts, purl the purl sts.
N3: Knit.
Repeat these two rounds until 56 total sts remain.

Foot
Round 1:
N1: Knit
N2: Knit the k sts, purl the p sts.
N3: Knit
Repeat Round 1 until foot measures 2"/5cm less than the length of your foot from heel to toe.

Toe Shaping
Round 1:
N1: Knit to last 3 sts, k2tog, k1.
N2: K1, Skp, knit to last 3 sts, k2tog, k1.
N3: K1, Skp, knit to end.
Round 2:
Knit across N1, N2, and N3.
Repeat Rnds 1–2 for 14 rounds total. (28 sts remain)
Rep Round 1 only until 16 sts remain, divided as follows:
N1: 4 sts
N2: 8 sts
N3: 4 sts

STITCH CHART
(Petal Lace Stitch)
(over a multiple of 28 sts)

28-st

Rep Rounds 1–14

Legend

│	Knit
▬	Purl
○	Yarn over
╲	Skp
╱	K2tog
⅄	Sk2p

FINISHING
- Place 4 sts from N3 onto N1. (8 sts on N1) Cut yarn, leaving a 12"/30.5cm tail.
- Holding N1 and N2 together, graft sts together from RS with Kitchener Stitch (see page 36.)
- Weave in ends. Block sock if desired.

DESIGN TIP
If you prefer, the Petal Lace patt can be worked over instep sts all the way up to the toe shaping.

MINI MESSENGER BAG

If you spend most of your time on the go but hate being weighed down by a bulky bag, this stylish shoulder bag is for you. Roomy enough to hold the essentials it is easy to master these stitches to create the bag's pretty patterning. The main body is knit beginner-friendly garter stitch and then finished off with a dainty lace flap. Silver rings support an extra-long strap so you can travel light.

SKILL LEVEL
Easy

SIZE
One size

FINISHED MEASUREMENTS
7"/17.5cm x 8"/20cm x 2"/5cm

YARN
1 cone of J.&P. Coats Crochet Nylon Thread (100% nylon, 5.8oz/164g = approx 150 yd/137m per cone) in #049 Country Blue OR approx 150 yd/137m nylon medium-weight yarn

MATERIALS
- Size 7 U.S.(4.5 mm) or size to obtain gauge
- 8"/20cm zipper in blue
- 1/2 yd (.46m) satin or lining fabric of your choice
- 2 Tandy Leather Factory rings #11506-00 OR 21" x 3/4"/2.5 x 1.875cm nickel-plated
- 2" x 5"/5.1 x 12.7cm plastic or buckram strip
- Tapestry needle for seaming and weaving the ends

GAUGE
18 sts = 4"/10cm over St st
Always take time to check your gauge.

PATTERN NOTE
The Base of the bag is formed between the Decrease and Increase Rows. The Body of the bag is knit one piece. The sides are first sewn and then the Base is sewn to the sides of the bag. A plastic or buckram strip will be stitched on the WS of the Base for stability.

SPECIAL ABBREVIATIONS
K2tog: Knit two stitches together.
Inc 1: Knit into front, then into back of stitch.

STITCH PATTERN
Mini Lace Stitch
(over a multiple of 2 sts plus 2 extra)
Row 1 (RS): K1, *yo, k1; rep from * to last st, k1.
Row 2 (WS): K1, purl across to last st, k1.
Row 3: K1, (k2tog) across to last st, k1.
Rows 4, 5, and 6: K1, *yo, k2tog; rep from * to last st, k1.
Rows 7 and 8: Knit across.
Rep Rows 1-8 for Sufiyana Lace Stitch patt.

BAG
Body
- Cast on 18 sts. Work in Mini Lace Stitch patt for 7 1/2"/18.75cm ending on row 8.
- **Next row:** (Inc 1) twice, (k1, inc 1) twice, k1, (inc 1) four times, (k1, inc 1) twice, k1, (inc 1) twice (30 sts).
- Work Garter st over 30 sts for 8"/20cm.

Decrease Rows
- **Next row:** Bind off 5 sts.
- Knit across. Turn. Bind off 5 sts.
- Work 20 sts in Garter st for 2"/5cm from bind off row.
- **Next row:** Cast on 5 sts, knit across. Turn. Cast on 5 sts knit across.

Increase Rows
Work in Garter st for 7"/17.5cm from the second cast on edge. Bind off all 30 sts.

HANDLE
CO 5 sts. Work in Garter St for 33"/84cm.

Handle Tab
(Make 2)
Cast on 3 sts. Work in Garter St for 3"/7.6cm.

FINISHING
- Lay purse Body on lining fabric. Trace the Body (do not include the lace flap), adding a 1/2"/1.25cm seam allowance and cut.
- Trace and cut plastic the same size as the 2"/5cm Base.
- Sew plastic to the Base of the bag on the WRONG side.
- Sew sides of lining, keeping the 7"/17.5cm opening unsewn.
- Lay bag on surface. Fold body of bag over, matching right sides together; without including the Flap. Stitch sides of bag just below the

STITCH CHART
(Mini Lace Stitch)
(over a multiple of 2 sts
plus 2 extra)

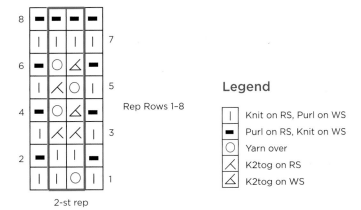

Rep Rows 1-8

2-st rep

Legend

	Knit on RS, Purl on WS
▬	Purl on RS, Knit on WS
○	Yarn over
⋋	K2tog on RS
⟋	K2tog on WS

lace Flap. Stitch the Base sides to the sides of bag; giving the bottom a flat base. Keep the 7"/17.5cm bag opening unsewn. Flip over so that the right side faces out.

• Place lining in the Body of the bag with WRONG sides together.

• Unzip the zipper and situate between lining and bag opening. End of zipper should be tucked in between lining and Body. Fold raw edges of lining towards the zipper edge and stitch. Stitch other side of zipper to Body.

• Place rings in between tabs and stitch in place.

• Place tabs on sides of purse and secure by stitching in place.

• Fold both sides of strap around metal rings. Sew side edges into place.

DESIGN TIP
A large ornamental button can be added to the bottom of the flap to secure and give accent your bag.

VINTAGE CAPELET

In the Victorian era, capelets served as elegant outerwear over formal dresses. Updated for today's woman, our version features a stylish pleat design that allows the knitted fabric to gracefully drape the shoulders. We selected delicate rib and lace stitches to emphasize the vintage look and to suit evening occasions.

SKILL LEVEL
Intermediate

SIZE
One size

FINISHED MEASUREMENTS
Length: 12½"/31.8cm
Width at top of capelet:
21"/53.3cm
Width of bottom of capelet:
45"/114.3cm

YARN
1 skein of Red Heart Luster
Sheen (100% acrylic, 4 oz/114g
= approx 335 yd/306m per
skein) in #0518 Lt. Mulberry OR
approx 335 yd/306m acrylic,
fine weight yarn

MATERIALS
• Size 5 U.S. (3.75mm) needles
  or size to obtain gauge
• Stitch markers
• Cable needle
• Tapestry needle for weaving
  in ends
• Brooch or pin

GAUGE
26 sts and 33 rows = 4"/10cm
over St st
Always take time to check
your gauge.

PATTERN NOTES
• There will be 8 panels of
  rib and 7 panels of lace.
• Stitches will decrease
  dramatically during the
  pleat row.

• Both chart and written
  instructions for Capelet Lace
  patt are provided. Choose
  the instruction method
  you prefer.

How to Pleat
• **Pleat knit st for Left Pleat:**
  Insert the RH ndl into the
  first st on the cable needle as
  if to knit. Then insert the RH
  ndl into the first st on the LH
  ndl as if to knit. Knit these 2
  stitches together. Drop both
  sts from cable needle
  and LH ndl.
• **Pleat knit st for Right Pleat:**
  Work as for Pleat knit st
  for Left Pleat above, except insert RH needle into
  LH needle st first, then into
  cable needle st, before working each st.
• **Pleat purl st for Left Pleat:**
  Insert the RH ndl into the
  first st on the LH ndl as if
  to purl. Then insert the RH
  needle into the first st on
  the cable needle as if to purl.
  Purl these 2 stitches together. Drop both sts from cable
  needle and LH ndl.
• **Pleat purl st for Right Pleat:**
  Work as for Pleat purl st
  for Left Pleat above, except
  insert RH needle into cable
  needle st first, then into LH
  needle st, before working
  each st.

SPECIAL ABBREVIATIONS
Pm: Place marker
K2tog: Knit 2
stitches together
S2kp: Slip 2 stitches. Knit next
stitch and pass the 2 slipped
stitches over the knit stitch
and off the needle.
Skp: Slip 1 stitch. Knit next
stitch and pass the slipped
stitch over the knit stitch and
off the needle.
Yo: Yarn over
8-st Left Pleat: Slip 8 sts to
cable needle and hold in front
of the next 8 lace sts.
Pleat the following sts:
K3, p1, k3, p1.
8-st Right Pleat: Slip 8 lace
sts to cable needle and hold
in back of the next 8 rib sts.
Pleat the following sts: p1, k3,
p1, k3.

STITCH PATTERNS
Capelet Lace Stitch
(over a multiple of 8 sts
plus 2 extra)
Rows 1 and 3 (RS): K1, *Skp,
(k1, yo) twice, k1, k2tog, k1;
rep from *.
Row 2 and all WS rows: Purl
Row 5: K1, *yo, Skp, k3, k2tog,
yo, k1; rep from *.
Row 7: K1, *k1, yo, Skp, k1,
k2tog, yo, k2; rep from *.
Row 9: K1, *k2, yo, S2kp, yo,
k3; rep from *.
Row 10: Rep Row 2.
Rep Rows 1–10 for Capelet
Lace Stitch patt.

STITCH CHART
(Capelet Lace Stitch)
(over a multiple of 8 sts plus 2 extra)

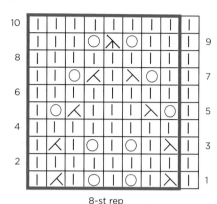

8-st rep

Rep Rows 1–10

Legend

Ⅰ	Knit on RS, Purl on WS
○	Yarn over
╱	K2tog
╲	Skp
⅄	S2kp

Seed Rib Stitch
(over a multiple of 4 sts plus 1 extra)
Row 1 (RS): P1, *k3, p1; rep from * to end.
Row 2 (WS): K2, *p1, k3; rep from * to last 3 sts, p1, k2.
Rep Rows 1-2 for Seed Rib Stitch patt.

CAPELET
CO 255 sts. Work *[17 sts in Seed Rib Stitch patt, pm, 17 sts in Capelet Lace Stitch patt, pm]; rep from * to last 17 sts, work 17 sts in Seed Rib Stitch patt. Continue in patts as established until 39 rows of Capelet Lace patt are complete, ending with a RS row.

Decrease Row (WS)
*[Work 17 sts in Seed Rib Stitch patt, p8, p2tog, p7]; rep from * to last 17 sts, work 17 sts in Seed Rib Stitch patt. (248 sts)

Pleat row (RS)
(P1, k3) twice, p1, *[8-st Left Pleat, 8-st Right Pleat, p1]; rep from * to last 9 sts, (p1, k3) twice, p1. (136 sts)

Decrease Row (WS)
K2, *[(p1, k3) 3 times, p1, k1, k2tog, k1]; rep from * to last 3 sts, p1, k2. (129 sts)
Work Rows 1-2 of Seed Rib Stitch patt until Capelet measures 12 1/2"/31.8cm from beginning. Bind off loosely in Seed Rib Stitch patt.

FINISHING
Weave in ends. Secure capelet with brooch or pin.

DESIGN TIP
If you prefer, you can add a buttonhole at desired spot., then attach button opposite buttonhole to secure your capelet.

KIMONO SHRUG

The comfortable elegance of a Chinese kimono was the inspiration for this simple and stylish kimono shrug. It is Knit in one piece using a simple lace stitch. Cotton blend yarn provides beautiful drape and the stitch pattern gives the impression that the piece was crocheted. Easy and quick to knit, this is a coverup fit for any occasion.

SKILL LEVEL
Easy

SIZE
One size

FINISHED MEASUREMENTS
10" x 36"/25 x 91.4cm

YARN
1 ball of Coats and Clark Aunt Lydia's Denim Quick Crochet (75% cotton/25% acrylic, approx 400 yd/366m per ball) in #1021 Linen OR approx 400 yd/366m cotton/acrylic blend, worsted-weight yarn

MATERIALS
- Size 8 U.S. (5mm) needles or size to obtain gauge
- Tapestry needle for attaching tie and weaving in ends
- Stitch markers

GAUGE
16 sts = 4"/10cm over St st
Always take time to check your gauge.

PATTERN NOTES
- Attach shrug according to schematic.
- Both chart and written instructions for Lace Stitch are provided. Choose the instruction method you prefer.
- For instructions on working I-cord, see page 32.

SPECIAL ABBREVIATIONS
Yo: Yarn over
Skop: Slip 1 stitch, knit 1 stitch, yo. Pass the slipped stitch over both the knit st and the yo and off the needle.
Drop yo: Drop the yo from the needle.

STITCH PATTERN
Lace Stitch
(over a multiple of 2 sts plus 1 extra)
Row 1 (RS): K1, *yo, Skop; rep from * across.
Row 2 (WS): *P2, drop yo; rep from *, end p1.
Row 3: K2, *yo, Skop; rep from * to last st, k1.
Row 4: P1, *p2, drop yo; rep from * to last 2 sts, p2.
Rep Rows 1–4 for Lace St patt.

SHRUG
Cast on 131 sts. Work in Lace St patt for 10"/25cm ending with a Row 2 or 4. Count 53 sts on needle, place marker, count 25 stitches, place marker.

Shaping
- **Next Row (RS):** Work in Lace St patt as established up to first marker. Place 53 sts just worked on hold. Bind off 25 sts, work remaining 53 sts in Lace St patt.
- Work even on this side of shrug in Lace St patt as established until shrug measures 20"/50cm from beg,

ending with a RS row. Bind off sts on WS.
- WS facing, rejoin yarn to remaining 53 sts and work next row of Lace St patt across. Continue even on this side of shrug in Lace St patt as established until this side measures same length as first side, ending with a RS row. Bind off 53 sts on WS.

FINISHING
Weave in ends. Block to measurements on schematic. Fold shrug as directed in schematic. Sew edges of folded piece together, beginning at side edge and ending 6"/15cm in from each side edge. Leave remaining 7"/17.5cm unsewn.

I – CORD EDGING
Attaching Cord
- Cast on 2 sts, leaving a 2"/5cm tail. Work in I-cord for 7 rows. Do not cut yarn. Slip 2 sts onto stitch holder. Take end of 2"/5cm tail and pull through edge of shrug sleeve, securing tightly to edge of sleeve.
- *[Slip 2 sts back onto needle, then with second needle, slip second st over the first st and off the needle, leaving 1 st on needle. Slip tip of same needle into the edge of sleeve 1"/2.5cm from the previous attachment point of I-cord. Pick up and knit 1 stitch (2 sts on ndl). Work

STITCH CHART
(Lace Stitch)
(over a multiple of 2 sts
plus 1 extra)

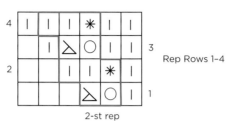

Rep Rows 1–4

2-st rep

Legend

	Knit on RS, Purl on WS
O	Yarn over
⟋	Skop
✳	Drop yo

---

in I-cord for 7 rows]; rep
from * around entire sleeve
edge, making sure each loop
is spaced 1"/2.5cm apart.
Repeat for other sleeve and
neck edge.

TIE
Cast on 5 sts. Work in Garter
Stitch (knit every row) until
177 ridges are complete. (354
rows) From the 30th ridge
on the tie, attach tie around
the lower edge of left front,
along the free lower edge of
back, and around lower edge
of right front, leaving last 30
ridges of tie free.

DESIGN TIP
Give the shrug a more
romantic look by attaching
a lace edging to the sleeves,
bodice front, and neckline.

SCHEMATIC

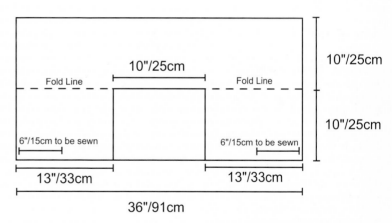

Fold Line   10"/25cm   Fold Line   10"/25cm

6"/15cm to be sewn   6"/15cm to be sewn   10"/25cm

13"/33cm   13"/33cm

36"/91cm

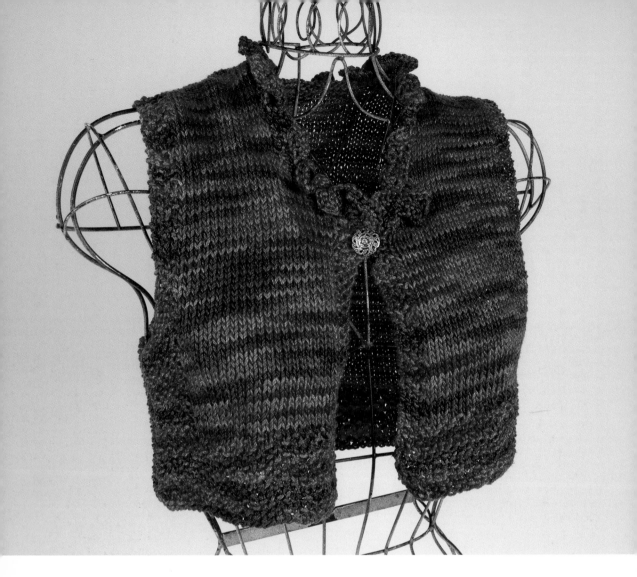

CROPPED VEST

If you are looking for a way to add a vivid splash of color and zest to
your closet, this cropped, ruffled vest will do the trick. Knit with a soft,
cotton-blend yarn in stockinette and seed stitches, it's a quick and easy
knit for beginning knitters.

SKILL LEVEL
Beginner

SIZE
Sizes Small (Medium, Large, Extra Large) to fit 32 (34, 36, 38)"/80 (85, 90, 95)cm bust
Shown in size Medium

FINISHED MEASUREMENTS
Length: 14 (14½, 15, 15½)"/35 (36, 37.5, 39)cm
To fit bust sizes: 32 (34, 36, 38)"/80 (85, 90, 95)cm

YARN
1 hank Schaefer Yarn Company Laurel (100% mercerized pima cotton yarn, 8oz = approx 400 yd/366m per hank) in Frida Kahlo OR approx 400 yd/366m cotton, worsted- weight yarn

MATERIALS
- Size 8 U.S.(5mm) needles or size to obtain gauge
- 1 button, ¾" (1.9cm) in diameter
- Tapestry needle for attaching ruffle and weaving in ends
- Stitch markers

GAUGE
18.5 sts = 4"/10cm over St st
Always take time to check your gauge.

PATTERN NOTES
- Stitches between markers will be worked in Stockinette stitch (Knit on RS, purl on WS). Stitches on the edges will be worked in Seed Stitch throughout.
- Instructions are given for size S, with sizes (M, L, XL) in parentheses. When only one number is given, it pertains to all sizes. Take care to follow the set of instructions that pertains to your chosen size throughout.

SPECIAL ABBREVIATIONS
Pm: Place marker
BO: Bind off
Inc 1: Increase by knitting into front, then into the back of the same stitch before slipping it off the needle.
Inc 2: Increase by knitting into the front, back, and then front of the same stitch before slipping it off the needle.

STITCH PATTERN
Seed Stitch
Row 1 (RS): *K1, p1; rep from * across.
Row 2: Purl the knit sts and knit the purl sts.
Rep Row 2 for Seed St.

VEST
Left Front
- Cast on 37 (39, 41, 43) sts. Work in Seed St for 15 rows.
- **Row 16 (RS):** Work 12 (14, 16, 18) sts in Seed St, pm, knit across to last 4 sts, work 4 sts in Seed St.
- **Row 17 (WS):** Work 4 sts in Seed St, pm, purl across to last 12 (14, 16, 18) sts, work 12 (14, 16, 18) sts in Seed St.
- Rep Rows 16–17 until left front measures 5½ (6, 6½, 7)"/ 13.75 (15, 16.25, 17.5)cm from beg, ending with a WS row.

Armhole Shaping
- **Next row (RS):** Bind off 3 (3, 4, 4) sts (armhole edge), work in patts as established to end. (34, 36, 37, 39 sts remain)
- Work 1 row even. Bind off 2 (2, 3, 3) sts at beg of next row. (32, 34, 34, 36 sts remain)
- Work 1 row even. Bind off 1 (2, 2, 2) sts at beg of next row. (31, 32, 32, 34 sts remain)
- Bind off 1 st at same edge (every 4th row) 2 (2, 2, 3) times. (29, 30, 30, 31 sts remain) Work even in patts as established until left front measures 8 (8½, 9, 9½)"/ 20 (21.25, 22.5, 23.75)cm from beg, ending with a RS row.

Neck Shaping
- On WS, BO 5 (6, 6, 7) sts at beg of next row. (24 sts remain)

- Continue in patts, BO 1st at neck edge on every 4th row until 19 sts remain. Work even in patt as established until front measures 14 (14$^{1}/_{2}$ 15, 15$^{1}/_{2}$)"/35 (36.25, 37.5, 38.75)cm from beg, ending with a WS row.

Shoulder Shaping

Next row (RS): BO 9 sts, knit across.

Next row (WS): Purl across. BO remaining 10 sts.

Right Front

- CO 37 (39, 41, 43) sts. Work in Seed St for 15 rows.
- **Row 16 (RS):** Work 4 sts in Seed St, pm, purl across to last 12 (14, 16, 18) sts, work 12 (14, 16, 18) sts in Seed St.
- **Row 17 (WS):** Work 12 (14, 16, 18) sts in Seed St, pm, knit across to last 4 sts, work 4 sts in Seed St.
- Rep Rows 16–17 until right front measures 5$^{1}/_{2}$ (6, 6$^{1}/_{2}$, 7)"/ 13.75 (15, 16.25, 17.5)cm from beg, ending with a RS row.

Front Armhole Shaping

- **Next row (WS):** Bind off 3 (3, 4, 4) sts (armhole edge). (34, 36, 37, 39 sts remain)
- Work in patts as established to end.
- Work 1 row even. Bind off 2 (2, 3, 3) sts at the beg of next row. (32, 34, 34, 36 sts remain)

- Work 1 row even. Bind off 1 (2, 2, 2) sts at the beg of next row. (31, 32, 32, 34 sts remain)
- Bind off 1 st at same edge (every 4th row) 2 (2, 2, 3) times. (29, 30, 30, 31 sts remain)
- Work even in patts as established until right front measures 7$^{1}/_{2}$ (8, 8$^{1}/_{2}$, 9)"/18.75 (20, 21.25, 22.5)cm from beg, ending with a WS row.

Work Buttonhole

- **Next Row (RS):** Work 2 sts in Seed St, yo, k2tog (if next st is a purl st) or p2tog (if the next st is a knit st). Work in patts to end.
- **Next Row (WS):** Work in patts to last 4 sts, work last 4 sts in Seed St. Work even in patts as established until right front measures 8 (8$^{1}/_{2}$ 9, 9$^{1}/_{2}$)"/20 (21.25, 22.5, 23.75)cm from beg, ending with a WS row.

Neck Shaping

- On RS, BO 5 (6, 6, 7) sts at beg of next row. (24 sts remain)
- Continue in patts, BO 1st at neck edge on every 4th row until 19 sts remain. Work even in patt as established until front measures 14 (14$^{1}/_{2}$ 15, 15$^{1}/_{2}$)"/35 (36.25, 37.5, 38.75)cm from beg, ending with a RS row.

Shoulder Shaping

- **Next row (WS):** BO 9 sts, knit across.
- **Next row (RS):** Knit across.
- BO remaining 10 sts on WS.

Back

- Cast on 73 (77, 81, 85) sts. Work in Seed Stitch for 15 rows.
- **Row 16 (RS):** Work 12 (14, 16, 18) sts in Seed St, pm, knit across to last 12 (14, 16, 18) sts, work 12 (14, 16, 18) sts in Seed St.
- **Row 17 (WS):** Work 12 (14, 16, 18) sts in Seed St, pm, purl across to last 12 (14, 16, 18) sts, work 12 (14, 16, 18) sts in Seed St.
- Rep Rows 16–17 until back measures 5$^{1}/_{2}$ (6, 6$^{1}/_{2}$, 7)"/ 13.75 (15, 16.25, 17.5)cm cm from beg, ending with a WS row.

Back Armhole Shaping

- **Next row (RS):** Bind off 3 (3, 4, 4) sts at the beg of next 2 rows, working all other sts in patts as established. (67, 71, 73, 77 sts remain)
- Bind off 2 (2, 3, 3) sts at the beg of the next 2 rows, keeping other sts in patts. (63, 67, 67, 71 sts remain)
- Bind off 1 (2, 2, 2) sts at the beg of the next two rows, keeping other sts in patts. (61, 63, 63, 67 sts remain)

- Bind off 1 st at each armhole edge (every 4th row) 2 (2, 2, 3) times. (57, 59, 59, 61 sts remain)
- Work even in patts as established until back measures 14 (14½, 15, 15½)"/35 (36.25, 37.5, 38.75)cm from beg, ending with a WS row.

To Shape Shoulder
- **Next row:** BO 9 sts at beginning of next two rows. (39, 41, 41, 43 sts remain)
- BO 10 sts at beginning of next two rows. BO remaining 19 (21, 21, 23) sts.

Ruffle
With leftover yarn, cast on 91 (91, 110, 110) sts. Knit one row.
Next row: Inc 2 (2, 1, 1) stitches in each stitch across. 273 (273, 220, 220 sts)
Next row: Knit
Next row: Purl
Next row: Knit
Next row: BO all sts.

FINISHING
Block vest. Sew shoulder seams using Invisible Horizontal Seam (see page 36). Sew side seams using Mattress Stitch (see page 35). Sew cast-on edge of Ruffle to neck edge, beg at right front neck shaping, going up right front and around back neck opening, then down left front to beg of left front neck shaping, gathering or easing to fit as needed. Attach button to

Seed St band of left front at front opening, opposite right front buttonhole.

DESIGN TIP
If you prefer, you can make this vest without the buttonhole and secure with a pin instead.

SCHEMATIC

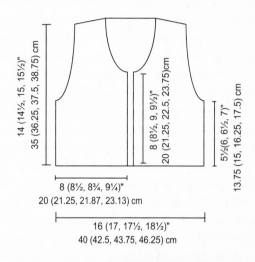

14 (14½, 15, 15½)"
35 (36.25, 37.5, 38.75) cm

8 (8½, 9, 9½)"
20 (21.25, 22.5, 23.75)cm

5½(6, 6½, 7)"
13.75 (15, 16.25, 17.5) cm

8 (8½, 8¾, 9¼)"
20 (21.25, 21.87, 23.13) cm

16 (17, 17½, 18½)"
40 (42.5, 43.75, 46.25) cm

CLIMBING ROPE PONCHO

Experienced knitters will be delighted to put their skills on display in this versatile poncho. Climbing cable ropes and diagonal cable stitches are knit in four triangular panels that are finished off with a delicate picot edging. If you're looking to keep yourself toasty warm in the cold winter months, taking the time to knit this poncho will be well worth the challenge. It's almost impossible to believe it was knit from just one ball of yarn!

SKILL LEVEL
Experienced

SIZE
One size

FINISHED MEASUREMENTS
Length from neck to edge:
19"/47.5 cm
Circumference around lower
edge: 48"/120cm

YARN
1 skein of Lion Brand Yarn
Fishermen's Wool (100%
pure virgin wool, 8oz/229g
= approx 465 yd/425m per
skein) in color #098 Natural
OR approx 465 yd/425m wool,
worsted-weight yarn.

MATERIALS
• Size 9 U.S. (5.5mm) straight
  and 16" circular needles OR
  size to obtain gauge
• Cable needle
• Tapestry needle
• Stitch markers

GAUGE
16 sts and 22 rows = 4"/10cm
over St st
Always take time to check
your gauge.

PATTERN NOTES
• The poncho is knit in four
  separate panels and then
  sewn together.
• Both chart and written
  instructions for Stacked
  Cable Stitch patt (Chart A)

are provided. Choose the
instruction method
you prefer.
• Instructions for Twisted
  Cable Rib patt (Chart B) are
  provided in chart form only.

SPECIAL ABBREVIATIONS
Spp: Slip 1 stitch, purl next
stitch. Pass the slipped stitch
over the purl stitch and off the
needle.
Skp: Slip 1 stitch, knit next
stitch. Pass the slipped stitch
over the knit stitch and off the
needle.
P2tog: Purl 2 stitches
together.
K2tog: Knit 2 stitches
together.
3-st left knit cable: Sl 2 sts to
cn and hold to front of work,
p1, k2 from cn.
3-st right knit cable: Sl 1 sts to
cn and hold to back of work,
k2, p1 from cn.
4-st right cable: Sl 2 sts to cn
and hold to back of work, k2,
k2 from cn.
4-st left cable: Sl 2 sts to cn
and hold to left of work, k2, k2
from cn
6-st right cable: Sl 3 sts to
cable needle and hold to
back of work, k3, k3 from
cable needle.
6-st left cable: Sl 3 sts to
cable needle and hold to
front of work, k3, k3 from
cable needle.

STITCH PATTERNS
C2-st Rib Stitch
(over a multiple of 4 sts,
worked in rounds for
turtleneck)
Rnd 1: *K2, p2; rep from *
around.
Rnd 2: K the knit sts, p the
purl sts.
Rep Rnd 2 for 2-st Rib St patt.

Stacked Cable Stitch
(over a multiple of 24 sts
plus 2 extra)
See Chart A on Page 99.
Row 1 (RS): P2, *k2, p2, (k6,
p2) twice, k2, p2; rep from *
to end
Row 2 and all WS rows: K the
knit sts, p the purl sts.
Row 3: P2, *k2, p2, 6-st right
cable, p2, 6-st left cable, p2,
k2, p2; rep from * to end.
Row 5: Rep Row 1
Row 6: Rep Row 2
Rows 7-24: Rep (Rows 1–6) 3
more times.
Row 25: P2, * k6, p2, (k2, p2)
twice, k6, p2; rep from *
to end.
Row 27: P2, *6-st left cable,
p2, (k2, p2) twice, 6-st right
cable, p2; rep from * to end.
Row 29: Rep Row 25
Row 30: Rep Row 2
Rows 31-48: Rep (Rows
25–30) 3 more times.
Work Rows 1–48 once, then
Rows 1–23 once more for
Stacked Cable St patt.

Twisted Cable Rib
See Chart B, Pages 100 and 101.

PONCHO
Stacked Cable Section (Section A)
(Make 2)
Cast on 50 sts. Work Stacked Cable St patt Rows 1–48, then Rows 1–23 once more, and at the same time, dec 1 st on each side (every 5 rows) throughout, keeping remaining sts in Stacked Cable St patt as established.
BO remaining 22 sts.

Twisted Cable Rib Section (Section B)
(Make 2)
Cast on 80 sts. Begin Twisted Cable Rib patt (Chart B). Work Rows 1–71 once. Bind off 20 sts.

Finishing
Block pieces. Sew together according to schematic: With RS facing, sew side edges of sections together as follows: A, B, A, B, turning B sections upside down as shown in schematic. Then sew the side edges of the outermost sections together, forming a cone.

TURTLENECK
RS facing, using circular needle, pick up and knit 116 sts around entire neck edge (narrow end of cone). Place marker to mark beg of round. Work in rounds of 2-st Rib Stitch patt until turtleneck measures 5½"/14cm. Bind off in Rib patt.

Picot Edging
Cast on one stitch. RS of Poncho facing you, insert RH ndl into lower edge of poncho. *[Pick up and knit 1 st. (2 sts) Slip first st over second st. (1 st) Slip st to LH ndl. Cast on 2 more sts. (3 sts). K3 sts. Slip 2 sts over last st on ndl. (1 st). Insert needle into 3rd edge stitch]; rep from * around entire lower edge, always picking up sts 3 sts apart. Bind off.

Finishing
Weave in ends.

DESIGN TIP
If you prefer, you can work the picot edging on the neck edge instead of knitting the turtleneck.

SCHEMATIC

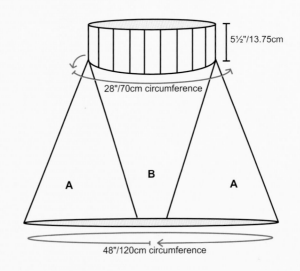

5½"/13.75cm

28"/70cm circumference

B

A   A

48"/120cm circumference

STITCH CHARTS

CHART A
(Stacked Cable Stitch)
(over a multiple of 24 sts plus 2 extra)

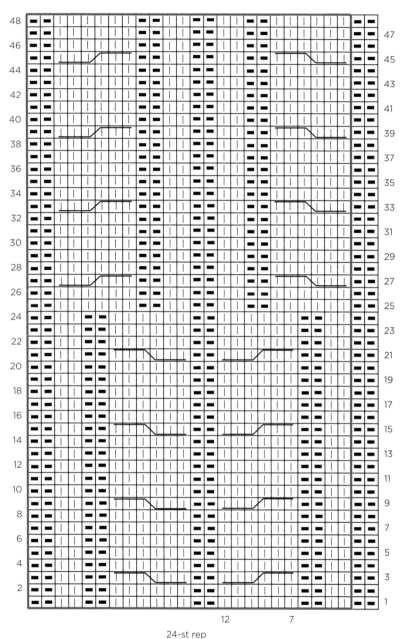

24-st rep

Legend

I	Knit on RS, Purl on WS
▬	Purl on RS, Knit on WS
	6-st right cable
	6-st left cable

CHART B:
(Twisted Cable Rib Stitch)
(80 sts, decreased to 20 sts)

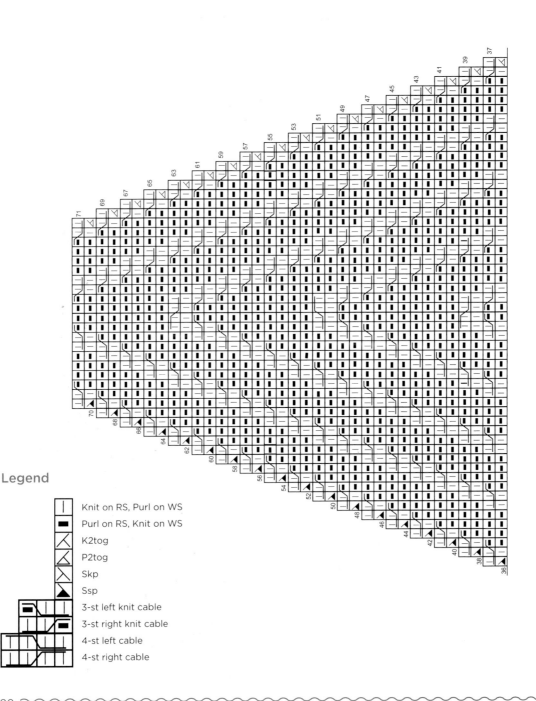

Legend

Knit on RS, Purl on WS	
Purl on RS, Knit on WS	
K2tog	
P2tog	
Skp	
Ssp	
3-st left knit cable	
3-st right knit cable	
4-st left cable	
4-st right cable	

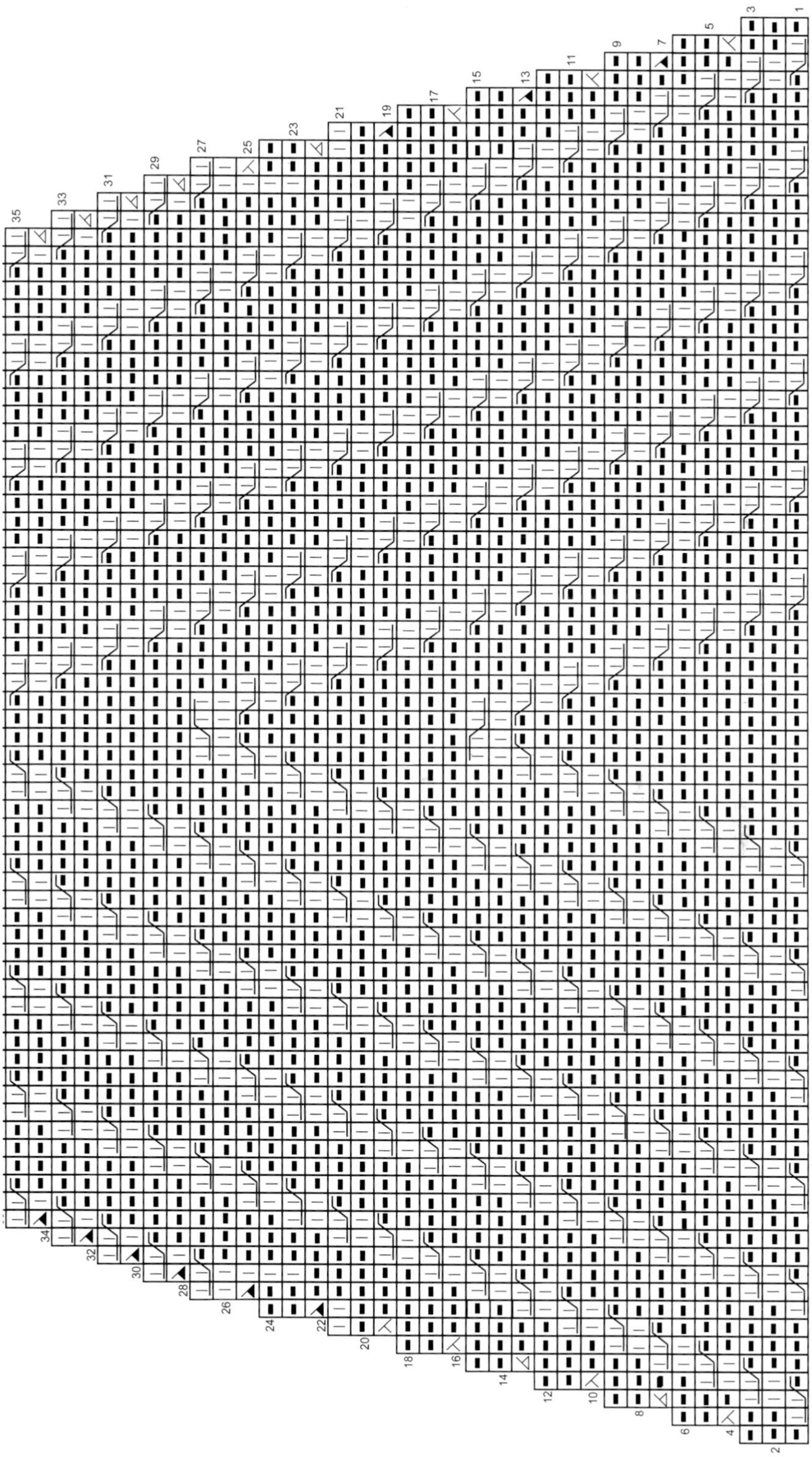

TURKISH WRAP

Turkey, with its rich heritage has given much to the world in the areas of art and architecture. Using the Turkish ribbed pattern, we designed this shawl, which represents the subtle beauty of the ripples of the Mediterranean Sea set against the undulating mountains of Turkey. This shawl was knit with the softest alpaca wool-blend yarn in chocolate brown, which leaves any wearer the impression of a cool day and warm night under the Turkish skies.

SKILL LEVEL
Easy

SIZE
One size

FINISHED MEASUREMENTS
12" x 60"/30.5 x 152cm, blocked

YARN
1 hank of Joseph Galler Prime Alpaca (100% superfine alpaca, 8 oz/229g = approx 665 yd/608m per hank) in Chocolate OR approx 665 yd/608m superfine alpaca sport weight yarn.

MATERIALS
- Size 6 U.S. (4mm) or size to obtain gauge
- Tapestry needle

GAUGE
24 sts = 4"/10cm over St st
Always take time to check your gauge.

PATTERN NOTES
- The wrap will shape automatically as you knit. The wrap is knitted in alternating patterns.
- Both charts and written instructions for Left-Slant Turkish Rib (Chart A), Right-Slant Turkish Rib (Chart B), and Lace Edging (Chart C) are provided. Choose the instruction method you prefer.
- Charts A, B, and C begin with a WS row. If using Charts, take care to work WS rows (including Row 1) from left to right, and RS rows from right to left.

SPECIAL ABBREVIATIONS
Skp: Slip 1 stitch, knit next stitch. Pass the slipped stitch over the knit stitch and off the needle.
S2kp: Slip 2 stitches. Knit next stitch and pass the 2 slipped stitches over the knit stitch and off the needle.
P2tog: Purl 2 stitches together.
K2tog: Knit 2 stitches together.
Yo: Yarn over
Pbss: Purl next st, slip back to LH needle. Slip second stitch on LH needle over the purl st and off the needle. Keeping yarn in front of needle, slip purl st to RH needle.

STITCH PATTERNS
Left-Slant Turkish Rib
(over a multiple of 2 sts)
See Chart A on page 104.
Row 1 (WS): P1, *yo, Pbss; rep from * to last st, p1.
Row 2 (RS): K1, *Skp, yo; rep from * to last st, k1.
Rep Rows 1–2 for Left-Slant Turkish Rib patt.

Right-Slant Turkish Rib
(over a multiple of 2 sts)
See Chart B on page 104.
Row 1 (WS): P1, *p2tog, yo, rep from * to last st, p1.
Row 2 (RS): K1, *yo, k2tog; rep from * to last st, k1.
Rep Rows 1–2 for Right-Slant Turkish Rib patt.

Lace Edging
(over a multiple of 6 sts plus 1 extra)
See Chart C on page 104.
Row 1 (WS): Purl
Row 2 (RS): K1, *yo, k1, S2kp, k1, yo, k1; rep from * to end.
Work (Rows 1–2) 3 times total for Lace Edging patt.

WRAP
Cast on 64 stitches. Knit one row. *[Work Left-Slant Turkish Rib patt over all sts for 18 rows, then work Right-Slant Turkish Rib patt over all sts for 8 rows, then work Left-Slant Turkish Rib patt over all sts for 8 rows, then work Right-Slant Turkish Rib patt over all sts for 18 rows]; rep from * 6 times more. Bind off.

Lace Edging
Make 2. Cast on 61 sts. Work Lace Edging patt for 6 rows. Bind off on WS.

FINISHING
Attach Lace Edging to narrow ends of wrap. Weave in ends. Block wrap.

STITCH CHARTS

CHART A
(Left-Slant Turkish Rib)
(over a multiple of 2 sts)

Rep Rows 1-2

2-st rep

CHART B
(Right-Slant Turkish Rib)
(over a multiple of 2 sts)

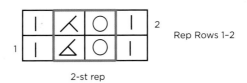

Rep Rows 1-2

2-st rep

CHART C
(Lace Edging) (over a
multiple of 6 sts
plus 1 extra)

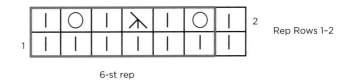

Rep Rows 1-2

6-st rep

Legend for
Charts A, B, and C

	Knit on RS, Purl on WS
A	Pbss
O	Yarn over
人	Skp
心	P2tog
人	K2tog
人	Sk2p

DESIGN TIP
Adding fringes to the remaining edges will give this wrap a
western look!

SOFT INDIGO LACE SHAWL

This light lace shawl recalls the cool scented breeze of a summer evening. Easily tackled by any intermediate knitter, this alpaca/silk blend wrap, delightfully soft and feather-light to the touch. Intricately knitted with a lace leaf interior and bordered with a pretty arrowhead lace stitch, it's perfect for draping over a romantic summer dress.

SKILL LEVEL
Intermediate

SIZE
One size

FINISHED MEASUREMENTS
14" x 65"/35.5 x 165cm

YARN
1 hank of Alpaca With A Twist Fino (70% baby alpaca/ 30% silk, 100g = approx 875 yd/800m per hank) in #1001 Duchess Blue OR approx 875 yd/800m baby alpaca/silk blend, superfine weight yarn in light blue

MATERIALS
• Size 3 U.S. (3.25mm) or size to obtain gauge
• Tapestry needle

GAUGE
28 sts = 4"/10cm over St st
Always take time to check your gauge.

PATTERN NOTES
• After completing the Soft Indigo Lace and Arrowhead Lace Stitch patts, pick up 109 stitches from the cast-on edge and repeat Arrowhead Lace Stitch patt.
• Both charts and written instructions for Soft Indigo Lace Stitch patt (Chart A) and Arrowhead Lace Stitch patt (Chart B) are provided. Choose the instruction method you prefer.
• Throughout, keep first and last 4 sts of each row in Garter St (knit every row) for border. These 4 sts at each edge are not included in Charts.

SPECIAL ABBREVIATIONS
K2tog: Knit two stitches together.
P2tog: Purl 2 stitches together.
P2togtbl: Purl 2 stitches together through their back loops.
Skp: Slip 1 stitch, knit next stitch. Pass the slipped stitch over the knit stitch and off the needle.
Sk2p: Slip 1 stitch, knit 2 stitches together. Pass the slipped stitch over the two stitches knit together and off the needle.

STITCH PATTERNS
Soft Indigo Lace Stitch
(multiple of 20 sts plus 1 extra)
See Chart A on page 108.
Row 1 (RS): *K1, yo, Skp, k4, Skp, yo, k3, yo, k2tog, k4, k2tog, yo; rep from * to last st, k1.
Rows 2, 4, 6: Purl
Row 3: *K2, yo, Skp, k4, Skp, yo, k1, yo, k2tog, k4, k2tog, yo, k1, rep from * to last st, k1.
Row 5: *K3, yo, Skp, k11, k2tog, yo, k2, rep from * to last st, k1.
Row 7: *K4, yo, Skp, k9, k2tog, yo, k3, rep from * to last st, k1.
Row 8: P1, *yo, p4, p2tog, p7, p2togtbl, p4, yo, p1; rep from * to end.
Row 9: *K2, yo, k4, Skp, k5, k2tog, k4, yo, k1; rep from * last st, k1.
Row 10: P1, *p2, yo, p4, p2tog, p3, p2togtbl, p4, yo, p3; rep from * to end.
Row 11: *K4, yo, k4, Skp, k1, k2tog, k4, yo, k3; rep from * last st, k1.
Rows 12, 14, 16, and 18: Purl.
Row 13: *K2, yo, k2tog, k4, k2tog, yo, k1, yo, Skp, k4, Skp, yo, k1, rep from * to last st, k1.
Row 15: *K1, yo, k2tog, k4, k2tog, yo, k3, yo, Skp, k4, Skp, yo, rep from * to last st, k1.
Row 17: *K6, k2tog, yo, k5, yo, Skp, k5, rep from * to last st, k1.
Row 19: *K5, k2tog, yo, k7, yo, Skp, k4, rep from * to last st, k1.
Row 20: P1, *p3, p2togtbl, p4, yo, p1, yo, p4, p2tog, p4; rep from * to end.
Row 21: *K3, k2tog, k4, yo, k3, yo, k4, Skp, k2; rep from * last st, k1.
Row 22: P1, *p1, p2togtbl, p4, yo, p5, yo, p4, p2tog, p2; rep from * to end.
Row 23: *K1, k2tog, k4, yo, k7, yo, k4, Skp; rep from * to last st, k1.
Row 24: Purl.
Rep Rows 1–24 for Soft Indigo Lace Stitch patt.

Arrowhead Lace Stitch
(over a multiple of 10 sts
plus 1 extra)
See Chart B on page 108.
Row 1 (RS): K1, *(yo, Skp)
twice, k1, (k2tog, yo) twice; rep
from * to last st, k1.
Row 2 (WS): Purl
Row 3: *K2, yo, Skp, yo, Sk2p,
yo, k2tog, yo, k1; rep from *
to last st, k1.
Row 4: Purl
Rep Rows 1–4 for Arrowhead
Lace Stitch patt.

SHAWL

Cast on 109 stitches.
Keeping 4 stitches at the
beginning and the end of each
row in Garter St (knit every
row), begin the Soft Indigo
Lace patt over center 101 sts.
Work in patts as established
until shawl measures 34"/86.4
cm. Keeping 4 sts each edge
in Garter St as before, begin
working Arrowhead Lace patt
over center 101 sts until shawl
measures 49"/124.5cm. Work
4 rows in Garter St. Bind off
all stitches loosely. RS facing,
pick up and knit 109 stitches
from cast-on edge of shawl.
Keeping 4 sts at each edge in
Garter St, and beg with Row 2
of Arrowhead Lace patt, work
Arrowhead Lace patt over
center 101 sts. Continue working in patts as established until
shawl measures 64½"/163.8
cm total from end to end.
Work 4 rows in Garter St. Bind
off all stitches loosely.

FINISHING

Weave in ends. Block severely.

DESIGN TIP

For a brilliant look, add
contrasting colored beads
to the Soft Indigo Lace
Stitch section.

STITCH CHARTS

CHART A
(Soft Indigo Lace Stitch)
(over a multiple of 20 sts
plus 1 extra)

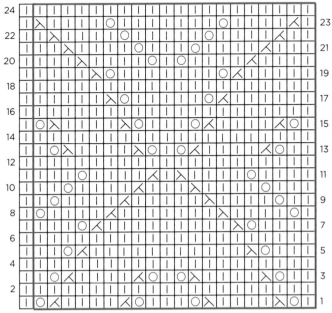

Rep Rows 1-24

20-st rep

Legend for Chart A

I	Knit on RS, Purl on WS
O	Yarn over
⋋	Skp on RS, P2togtbl on WS
⋌	K2tog on RS, P2tog on WS

CHART B
(Arrowhead Lace)
(multiple of 10 sts plus
1 extra)

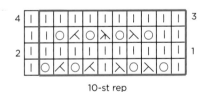

Rep Rows 1-4

10-st rep

Legend for Chart B

I	Knit on RS, Purl on WS
O	Yarn over
⋋	Skp
⋌	K2tog
⋏	Sk2p

SUPPLIERS

If you cannot find the yarn or craft supplies at your local store, you can contact these wholesalers that will provide you information on finding their products in a store near you.

YARN

Alpaca With A Twist
4272 Evans Jacobi Road
Georgetown, IN 47122
(866) 37-TWIST
www.alpacawithatwist.com

Berroco, Inc.
14 Elmdale Road.
PO Box 367
Uxbridge, MA 01569
www.berroco.com

Brown Sheep Co., Inc.
100662 County Road 16
Mitchell, NE 69357
(308) 635-2198
www.brownsheep.com

Coats & Clark
Consumer Services
P.O. Box 12229
Greenville, SC 29612-0229
(800) 648-1479
www.coatsandclark.com

Colinette Yarns
Distributed by Unique
Kolours
28 N. Bacton Hill Rd.
Malvern, PA 19355
(610) 644-4885
www.uniquekolours.com
www.colinette.com

Joseph Galler Yarns
5 Mercury Avenue
Monroe, N.Y. 10950
(800) 836-3314

Lion Brand Yarns
135 Kero Road
Carlstadt, NJ 07072
800-258-YARN
www.lionbrand.com

Rowan Yarns
Distributed by
Westminster Fibers
4 Townsend West, Unit 8
Nashua, NH 03063
(603) 886-5041
www.knitrowan.com

Schaefer Yarn Company
3514 Kelly's Corners Road
Interlaken, NY 14847
(607) 532-9452
www.schaeferyarn.com

S. R. Kertzer Limited
50 Trowers Road
Woodbridge, ON L4L 7K6
Canada
(800) 263-2354
www.kertzer.com

Tahki•Stacy Charles, Inc.
70-30 80th St., Bldg 36
Ridgewood, NY 11385
(800) 338-YARN
www.tahkistacycharles.com

BEADS

Pure Allure
4005 Avenida De La Plata
Oceanside, CA 92056
(800) 536-6312
www.pureallure.com

Creativity Inc.
Blue Moon Beads and
Westrim Crafts
7855 Hayvenhurst Avenue
Van Nuys, CA 91406
(800) 727-2727
www.westrimcrafts.com
www.bluemoonbeads.com

BUCKLES AND PURSE HARDWARE

BagWorks Inc.
Attn: Customer Service
3301-C South
Cravens Road
Fort Worth, TX 76119
(800) 365-7423
www.bagworks.com

M & J Trimming
1008 6th Avenue (between
37th and 38th Streets)
New York, New York 10018
(800) 9-MJTRIM
www.mjtrim.com

Tandy Leather Factory, Inc.
3847 East Loop 820 South
Fort Worth, TX 76119
(800) 433-3201
www.tandyleather.com

WIRE

Artistic Wire
752 North Larch Avenue
Elmhurst, IL 60126
(630) 530-7567
www.artisticwire.com

INDEX